Islands

on the

Fringe

A Year of Micronesian Waves and Wanderers

ISLANDS ON THE FRINGE:
A Year of Micronesian Waves and Wanderers

S. Jacques Stratton

Published by PhantaSea Books, Honolulu, Hawaii

Cover design by FatGraffix Studios, based on proprietary
photographs provided by the author

ISBN-13:   978-0-692-19284-9

Library of Congress Control Number: 2018963880

snacks, and trinkets. A computer magazine warns of the dangers of the "Y2K" bug, while a tabloid rack regales me with headlines about Bill Clinton's Oval Office escapades. Browsing further, I encounter a set of guidebooks to the Pacific islands. Among the titles, I find a guide to Micronesia, which I purchase along with several bags of trail mix. Suitably provisioned, I continue my trek through the airport.

Toward the outlying gates, doorways to routes less-traveled, the bustle of families and tourists gives way to rugged wayfarers whose slow saunter suggests acclimation to island time. At the gate for Continental Micronesia, I take a seat, open a bag of trail mix, and survey the handful of characters that lounge on a bench by the window. Stifling a yawn, a sloucher, his bloodshot eyes veiled by heavy lids, gives me a quick once-over. The bold letters of his T-shirt form a particularly stentorian version of the Guamanian greeting "Hafa Adai!" His buddies scowl at my trail mix as they jab plastic forks into a communal can of Spam. Outside the window, a 727 nests upon the tarmac, awaiting pre-flight maintenance. Relaxing with my snack, I arrange my duffel bag as a pillow, stretch out upon the row of seats, and settle in to some reading. *"The term Micronesia,"* the guidebook begins, *"means small islands, and refers to a vast region of the Pacific. From the Line Islands in the east to Palau in the west, thousands of low-lying coral atolls mix with an occasional lush, cloud-draped volcanic peak. . ."* The words blur; lulled by the warmth and humidity, I succumb to drowsiness.

A gruff voice startles me awake.

"Excuse me, did you drop this?"

Rubbing sleep from my eyes, I note the first hints of dawn outside. Before me, an outstretched arm holds my guidebook, which apparently had fallen to the floor. Behind the arm, a Hawaiian-shirted shoulder leads to a lined, tan face, where I see my reflection in a pair of Maui Jim sunglasses.

4

fashion and lava-lava skirts. As I watch the last boarders hand their tickets to the gate attendant, a reminder of my own journey comes to mind, and for an introspective moment, I ponder several months' worth of decisions, blunders, and resolutions that bring me to sip beer by a boarding gate at the crossroads of the Pacific.

Just a few months prior, my engagement to a girl I met in graduate school began to unravel. My beach-oriented lifestyle, barely supported from the income I earned as a part-time college English instructor, grew increasingly at odds with my fiancée's cosmopolitan cravings. Discrepancy turned to drama as we made our honeymoon plans. I envisioned frolicking on a palm-fringed island; she envisioned lounging in an haute hotel. I wanted to experience a south Pacific kava ceremony; she wanted to taste Tuscan wine. Therapy, started with serious intent, yielded hollow hopes and resentment. Meanwhile, I found salt-water solace in surfing, an escape-turned-obsession. While the wedding plans fell apart, my plan for a Pacific journey came together.

Now, fingering my teaching contract, I review the results of that plan. Embossed with the outrigger logo of the College of Micronesia, the document, effective August 1999, outlines the terms of a new life. Beer in hand, I review the compensatory details: paid airfare; shipping for one ton of belongings; a housing stipend; and a salary sufficient for basic comfort. To these perquisites I add the college's location: a tropical island, whose coral confines promise all the features I previously hoped to find on a honeymoon with my ex-fiancée. Reassured by the review, I drain my beer, place my contract in my jeans pocket, and leave a tip that generates a reluctant "Mahalo" from the bartender, who quickly returns his attention to the day's baseball highlights. Unsure if broadcast news even reaches my destination, I let my gaze linger on the T.V., and continue along the walkway.

After several storefronts, I come upon a magazine shop that lures me inside with its eclectic inventory of reading material,

3

last of the coast at Pt. Conception, where white caps on the ocean's surface denote a stiff breeze in the outer waters. The 767 adjusts its course subtly to the southwest, and for the five hours that remain before arrival in Honolulu, passengers transition to the tropics in a cocoon of recycled air and engine hum. Nestled in the night, a waxing moon, abetted by a few bold stars, frosts the airplane wings with a silver gleam. Nestled in their seats, travelers ignore the indomitable geography of the Pacific, its expanses seemingly tamed by jet engines inhaling eight miles of atmosphere a minute.

Making its landing approach, the plane skirts Diamond Head from the east, bringing the sparkle of Waikiki to the starboard windows. The pilot turns into the trade-wind, and Honolulu Airport's Reef Runway, a two-mile long ruler of black asphalt almost surrounded by moon-tinted sea, centers the plane's descent. The momentum of the flight dissipates as the plane taxis to its terminal, where, whispering through the margin between the exit ramp and the fuselage, the breath of the tropics greets travelers with a humid kiss.

For me, the flight concludes the first stage of a longer journey. Shouldering my duffel bag, I amble through the terminal, and bide my time before I seek the gate for Continental Micronesia's "island-hopper" — a 727 that offers a morning flight through four time zones to my final stop.

At a bar where the distractions of drinks and TV news provide solace to travelers-in-limbo, I settle into a counter seat. The bartender, his expression a gloss of pasted-on courtesy that comes from over-exposure to tedious tourists, places a Budweiser on a folded napkin. I bring the bottle to my lips and observe the activity at a nearby gate, where a Hawaiian Airlines flight, bound for American Samoa, begins to board. Bags brimming with the results of a Honolulu shopping excursion, the Samoans form a portly procession, their attire a cross-cultural pastiche of designer

2

Chapter 1: Across the Dateline

The jet accelerates into the August evening, banks toward the western horizon, and casts off the shackles of a Los Angeles heat wave. Escaping into the sunset, passengers watch fingers of fog massage the shoulders of the Channel Islands, observe an amber glow settle on the Santa Barbara ranches, and glimpse the

1

Islands on the Fringe:
A Year of Micronesian Waves and Wanderers

CONTENTS

"Had a glimpse of the gardens of Paradise been revealed to me I could scarcely have been more ravished with the sight"

—Herman Melville, *Typee*

DISCLAIMER

This book portrays the author's experience living and teaching on the island of Pohnpei during the 1999-2000 academic year. The narrative, a personal impression of that experience, recreates conversations, characters, and circumstances drawn from mind-states impaired, at times, by various influences, including, but not limited to, the sentimentality of nostalgic reminiscence, the haze of inebriation, and the eccentricity of personality disorder. Guided by the aesthetics of travelogue and memoir, the story presents details and descriptions intended to evoke the feeling of a moment in time rather than present a definitive account of such moments. Where appropriate, the author has endeavored to protect the privacy of individuals and the prestige of institutions.

For Q, who provided inspiration

For R.M., who helped me live the journey

For my parents, who nurtured a dreamer and remain always in my heart,

For Mer-maid, who put up with the writing,

For my family, friends, and acquaintances, companions of travels both brief and enduring,

And all who seek renewal on the magical margins of the world.

"Didn't mean to bother you," the friendly stranger smiles, handing me the guidebook. "Maybe you didn't want to lose it."

"Thanks," I say, fighting a yawn. "I must have dozed off."

"I'm Jeff Corson," he says, extending a handshake as he plops into the adjacent seat. "I could use a siesta myself, but Continental — Air Mike, as the regulars call it — likes to keep things on time. Here comes the gate attendant now."

Uniformed in Continental's dark blue and yellow, a woman opens the doors to the boarding ramp. The waiting passengers, now more numerous and scattered about the lounge area, begin to stir. The Spam-eaters nudge their heavy-lidded companion and find amusement in the reluctant way his groggy eyes adjust to the morning. Across from me, a mother fusses over her twin daughters, binding their pigtails with pink ribbons while the girls look wonderingly at the 727 outside the window. Meanwhile, cloistered by the gate attendant's desk, a clique of briefcase toters — hair close-cropped, shoes freshly polished — look every bit like G-men assembled for some secret purpose. Pondering their military seriousness, I recall that the flight makes a stop at Kwajalein, the tracking and research station for U.S. Air Force missile launches.

"Hi Jeff," I respond. "I'm Jacques. Sounds like you've flown this route before."

"I get around," he says, in the understated manner of a travel veteran confident in the self-evidence of his worldly sophistication. "What brings you to the island hopper?"

"Teaching," I reply simply, unsure how much of my backstory I should divulge to a stranger.

He nods, as though my answer confirms his own presupposition.

"I'm starting a contract with the College of Micronesia, National Campus," I explain.

"The Federated States? You better like rain, especially on

5

the high islands. I might have pegged you for a teacher."

"How so?" I inquire. My jeans, T-shirt, and flannel mark me as a nondescript traveler, or so I think.

"The more you travel to the Fringe, as I call it, the more you recognize certain character types," Jeff says. "Beyond Hawaii, travelers fit a standard recipe: two parts local islanders, and one-part Western hodge-podge, comprised of missionaries, government-affiliated types, and ex-pat professionals. Sometimes you'll find occasional bums like me. Vacationing tourists are a rarity."

The gate attendant announces the boarding and we line up to show our tickets. Wondering which faces represent the ingredients in Jeff's recipe, I look for an expression that might reveal the story behind the traveler. The one-way ticket in my pocket and the teaching contract in my bag bind me, it seems, to a cameo role in the narrative of Pacific castaways. As the line of passengers nudges me closer to the gate attendant, Jeff's words stir the butterflies in my stomach.

"And you? What brings you to the island hopper?" I inquire.

Lines of thought crease Jeff's face, and then erupt in a grin. "Indolence," he says.

"Indolence?"

"Indolence," he repeats, as if advertising a character trait. "At least, that's what my ex-wife would say."

"Seems a bit harsh," I comment. Familiar with Continental Micronesia's ticket prices, I opine that he must have some productive way to pay the bills.

"I run a boat-repair service," Jeff replies. "Sometimes yachties will fly me out to various islands to fix their vessels. Right now, a guy in Majuro, down in the Marshall Islands, has a marine diesel that he doesn't trust the local mechanics to fix."

"No kidding? Sounds like a good gig. . .or at least a good

adventure," I say.

"Tell that to my ex-wife" Jeff says. "She wished I was an attorney, working for a downtown firm. That's what folks with *ambition* do."

"Maybe you're too hard on yourself," I console. "Lots of people must envy a life like yours. Traveling around the Pacific, fixing boats. . ."

Jeff, inscrutable behind his sunglasses, lets my words hang in the air. "I get by," he eventually replies. "Anyway, don't worry about me. You should focus on your own situation."

"What do you mean? What's my situation?"

"Let me guess: one-way ticket, right?"

I nod.

"Well, there you go," he says.

We hand our tickets to the gate attendant, and then tramp along the boarding ramp. The flight appears half-full, and passengers, eager to lounge, switch from their initial seats to those with greater legroom. A few stains, evidence of past spilled drinks or sick stomachs, mark the carpet. I opt for a window seat near the tail. Jeff offers an effusively flirtatious greeting to the flight attendant, and then flops in the row behind me. A voice crackles over the intercom: "Welcome to Continental Micronesia Flight 957, with service to Majuro, Kosrae, Pohnpei, Chuuk and Guam. For your safety, please stow baggage securely in the overhead compartments." I fasten my seatbelt and look out the window. Glinting red and yellow, the fuselages of planes outside the distant main terminal reflect the dawn. I bring my sunglasses out of the pocket of my flannel. With a slight jolt, our 727 backs away from the gate and taxis to the runway. Nose to the trade-winds and engines surging, it takes off, banks, and races the sun's reflection southwest across a shimmering sea.

Cruising altitude brings us several hours of smooth flight, and then aligns us for an aerial dance with packs of exuberant

7

cumulonimbus, whose brawny shoulders the pilot skirts via subtly-timed course adjustments. Looking out the window, I feel suspended in a realm where sea and sky, each one reflecting the other's cerulean face, merge into a massive dome. The vastness of the tropical Pacific grows ominous, and I marvel at some of my guidebook's intriguing revelations: long before Europeans sailed beyond sight of land, Micronesian navigators used wave patterns, star alignments, and even the taste of fish to pluck tiny islands from the endless blue. We pass into the inter-tropical convergence zone, a region of equatorial air where the trade-winds fade, and thermals raise thunderclouds to great heights. One such cloud, wearing an anvil-shaped crown, probes the limits of sky above us.

"Sentinels of the sky!" Jeff suddenly barks. Switching to my row, he begins singing in a surprisingly melodic voice: *and I rise, like a bird/ in the haze, when the first rays/ touch the sky. . .*

"Pink Floyd," he says, grinning to the heads that turn our way.

"Pillow of Winds" I say, recognizing the song from my music-infused college years. "The last verse, with David Gilmour on vocals."

"You sure? Roger Waters sang most of their early stuff," Jeff asserts.

"I think that's a Gilmour track."

Pressing the call button, Jeff summons the stewardess. Cindy—as I infer from her name tag—comes down the aisle.

"Yes?" she inquires.

Jeff places a patronizing hand on her waist. "My friend Jacques and I have a dispute," he says.

"Oh? What can I do?" she asks, tolerating Jeff's hand, her smile that of a customer service veteran used to treating gentlemen and bozos with equal hospitality.

"You can tell us who sang vocals on Pink Floyd's 'Pillow of Winds.'"

8

"Pink Floyd? Who's he?"

"He's a band. . .you know. . . 'The Wall'? *We don't need no ed-yoo-ca-shun,*" Jeff prods.

"Sir, I don't know much pop trivia," she says. "Now, can I get you something? Pretzels, or maybe a drink?"

"I was hoping you might have something else on the menu," Jeff insinuates, dripping a little too much sleaze into a voice intended for charm.

Surmising that she was summoned for nothing more than Jeff's caddish ambitions, Cindy backs away, her index finger a-wag with admonishment. "Keep a leash on your friend," she tells me, her tone less sweet than her smile.

He's not really my friend, I mutter inwardly, miffed at being mistaken for an accomplice.

"She's such a cutie," Jeff whispers, his gaze following Cindy's posterior up the aisle. "She'd be more amenable after a nice dose of Vitamin A."

"Vitamin A?" I query.

"Alcohol," Jeff grins. "Every Pacific traveler should keep a bottle handy." By way of example, Jeff stands, rummages through the overhead bin, and presents a shiny thermos and two paper cups. "Vitamin A," he says, flashing me a conspiratorial wink as he fills the cups with amber liquid and passes one to me. "From the lab of Dr. Jack Daniels."

Raised in Los Angeles, a city well-known for charlatans and showmen, I retain a cynical view of Jeff's demeanor, and respond to Jeff's toast with only enough of a sip to be polite. The fact that Jeff singled me out as his traveling sidekick makes me a bit nervous, and I suspect that packed among his belongings a "Margaritaville" cap or shirt awaits, ready to promote participation in a drunken debauch. Trying to infer more about his character, I ask him about his journeys and favorite destinations, thinking preference of place a sign of personality.

"Well, there's a nice little massage parlor in Thailand that grabs my thoughts every now and then. Ever visited Thailand?"

"No."

"You mean, *not yet,*" he advises, caressing the rim of his whiskey cup. After a lengthy sip, he elaborates. "Most guys who venture to the Fringe eventually end up in a place where their dollars attract an excess of alcohol and women."

"I see."

"Your ex-pat life might start on an up-note, but sooner or later you wake up to find your ambitions eroded—by the relentless humidity, by alcoholics, and by girls who offer romance in exchange for ticket to the USA."

A patch of turbulence, theatrically timed to emphasize the doom-laden words, rattles the plane.

"Don't worry," Jeff soothes. "Life on the Fringe will alter your sensibilities. Once you acclimatize to the general degradation, you'll eat Spam straight from the can and call it breakfast!"

I recall the Guamanians at the airport gate, and my mind generates a zoom-lens vision of pink goo impaled on plastic forks. Though conveyed with a tone of comedy, the prediction resonates darkly. Since the demise of my relationship with my fiancée, my eagerness to go abroad rested on the presumption that my ex-pat life would outshine the smog-bound sufferings of life in Los Angeles. Now, less sanguine, I imagine myself destined for a beer-belly and laziness, forgotten by mainland friends dedicated to career and family. Suddenly my journey acquires connotations of distance I hadn't before considered, and I open my guidebook's map of the Pacific for a sense of perspective. The sporadic dots and squiggles indicative of terra firma resemble printing press mistakes, mere afterthoughts of ink rather than depictions of land. Among those depictions I find my own destination, and consider it a frail foundation for my ex-pat hopes. Reflexively, I reach for

Atoll islet, of the type that epitomizes the meaning of the term "Micronesia." Lonely sentinels surrounded by empty horizon, the islets--essentially coral rubble and salt-laden sand affixed to the higher portions of underlying reef--support a limited vegetation, sometimes consisting of a solitary palm tree. Viewed from the window of an airplane, they materialize from the blue and vanish in the slipstream.

my cup of "Vitamin A," and fortify myself with a fiery gulp.

With an eye tilted at my book, Jeff traces a finger along the dotted line that traverses the map from north to south, bisecting the Pacific and shifting in places to accommodate idiosyncratic national borders. "Ever crossed the dateline before?" he asks.

"First time," I confess.

"To the dateline!" Jeff proposes, giving our cups an enthusiastic refill. "In a little while we'll reach tomorrow, though we just started today!"

We drink to the dateline, and then raise successive toasts, as my companion finds on the map other items worthy of celebration. We drink to the Line Islands, where Jeff "bummed his way around" on a copra boat, gathering coconuts and developing his mechanic's craft. We drink to Western Samoa, where, I learn, the city of Apia hosts the South Pacific's best bar crawl, fueled by beer cheap and fresh from the Vailima brewery. By the time we drain the thermos, Jeff, nagged by nostalgia, directs a contemplative gaze out the window. "Should I have gone to college? Who can say?" he voices to no one in particular. "I just know I'm happy with my Vitamin A!" Raising his cup so the last amber drops drip on his tongue, Jeff gets up and heads to the restroom.

Down to the dregs of my own cup, I find myself numbed to my earlier anxiety. Then, peering out the window, I notice the blue water below acquire a turquoise hue, from which a string of atolls, sand ringing palms, suddenly emerges on a line extending northwest by southeast. Jeff, back from the restroom, leans over for a glimpse. "Marshall Islands, right on time," he says, checking his watch. "Those outer islands look like paradise, but Majuro's a dump. The pilot should announce our landing approach any time now."

The pilot does, and the plane begins its descent. A long,

12

Marshall Islands: a flotilla of green atolls anchored in the balmy blue. String a hammock between the palms and let the breeze bring a tropical dream

flat island comes in to view. Along its backbone runs a solitary main road, lined with cinder block buildings, their corrugated roofs flashing reflected sunlight. At the end of the island, a strip of sand, apparently raised from the sea expressly for runway support, awaits our arrival, like driftwood awaiting an albatross. We land between the foaming Pacific on one side and lapping lagoon on the other, and taxi to a group of cement huts. A faded

13

and splintered sign, with an over-inflated sense of importance, proclaims "Marshall Islands International Airport." Through the exit door comes an atmosphere thick enough to chew.

Jeff, departing, bids me good luck. "Take care, Jacques. Don't forget to take your Vitamin A!" With a dozen other passengers, he steps out into the sticky heat.

Warned by the flight attendants about our imminent resumption of flight, the continuing passengers and I remain in the plane. I stretch, use the restroom, and return to my seat, where I ponder this coral gangplank of an island — home, my guidebook tells me, to 60,000 inhabitants. At the runway's edge, the ocean waits patiently, assured with its eventual subjugation of the sand, whose elevation averages three feet.

The plane again takes to the air, but this time we fly only a few thousand feet above the water, the 220-mile jump to Kwajalein unworthy, apparently, of high-level flight. Soon, "Kwaj" greets us with a landscape like Majuro, only the buildings exude a seriousness of purpose made sterner by the island's restricted status. Domes, hangars, cement edifices, and facades without windows loom drab and mysterious, mute witnesses to the island's military activities. Uniformed personnel, like wardens of a secret society, come out to the plane. Briefcases in hand, the spit-and-polish government types from Honolulu troop to the exit door, which the flight attendants quickly shut behind them, as if even the atmosphere outside remains off-limits. During Operation Crossroads in 1946, my guidebook states, observers on this island could see the mushroom cloud from the atomic test at Bikini atoll, 240 miles to the north. Today, the only man-made clouds come from the exhaust of Continental 957, resuming its journey southwest.

Our next stop, Kosrae, provides a postcard portrait of a high island. Lush slopes rise steeply behind the fringing shore, their summits rushed by passing clouds. By the tarmac, a brightly

14

A runway view of Kwajelien. . .about as close as one can get without enlisting or working as a civilian contractor

painted pavilion, under a sign greeting travelers to "the mysterious paradise island," basks in afternoon heat. The flight attendants announce an hour's stopover, and, hat in hand, I opt for an exploration of the airport grounds. Most of the other passengers do likewise, and together we throng toward the pavilion. Under the shade of a corrugated roof, several local women and children manage an ad-hoc vending operation specializing in T-shirts, carvings, and assorted trinkets. A single customs officer, flashing a set of betel-stained teeth, waves us toward the vendors. They, in turn, wave us toward their merchandise.

"Sir, you like shell from Kosh-rye?" a small boy asks, tugging at my sleeve. He holds up a bracelet of polished shells.

Knowing that a purchase from the first hopeful child will

only inspire the ambitious salesmanship of the others, I shake my head and move on.   At the next vending stand, a woman with dark rheumy eyes like congealed molasses shows off an assortment of T-shirts, each depicting Kosrae's "sleeping lady mountain."   The sleeping lady, I discover, consists of an imaginative rendering of the island's volcanic spine. Viewed from a certain perspective, the peaks resemble the profile of a woman lying on her back.

"Does the sleeping lady ever awaken?" I jokingly ask of the woman.

She perks up, misinterpreting my attempt at humor as an interest in her wares. "Five dollars for shirt!" she chants.

As the throng crowds around, the boy, shrill-voiced, promotes his shells, and the odor of sweat permeates the air. A swarm of flies, previously content to circle the rafters, now makes bold forays toward us. Cramped by the pavilion's increasingly stifling atmosphere, I meander to a grassy promontory and find a non-claustrophobic view of the harbor. Daydreaming in the afternoon breeze, a solitary freighter lies at anchor. Whispers of wind sigh around my ears, gather strength, and blow my hat from my head. As I stoop to retrieve it, a sudden gust pushes it toward the harbor. Muffled laughter comes from the direction of the pavilion. I see a group of teenagers lounging against a wall, amused by my battle with the breeze. Doubling my effort, I make a successful grab for my hat, and raise my arms in mock victory, eliciting further grins from the teens.

"Where you from, meeshter?" asks a boy wearing a threadbare AC/DC t-shirt.

"California," I say, approaching my interrogators, who, by posture and personality, fit the profile of local youth engaged in the eternal adolescent pastime of loitering.

"My auntie live in U-S," volunteers another. "Eesh dat near Cal--Cali--where you from?"

"You could say that," I reply. Suddenly professorial, I elaborate: "In fact, California is one of the fifty states that comprise the U.S."

Eyes glazed, they process the information, then return to their lounging, passing around a plastic baggie, from which they each take a round nut about the size of a jumbo green olive. From another baggie they obtain a substance like salt crystals (lime powder, I later learn). After drizzling the crystals on the nuts, the

Kosrae Harbor, with portion of the "sleeping lady" mountains in the background. Typical of Micronesian high islands, Kosrae enjoys the lushness that comes from good soil and abundant water. Unfortunately, Edenic environs conferred little protection from the European diseases that, introduced by whalers and castaways, nearly wiped out the island population during the 1800s. For surf-minded travelers, Kosrae's historical significance dates back to the 1980's, when a National Geographic photo revealed lines of swell wrapping around the reef at Airport Point— situated on a promontory opposite the harbor—helping to put Micronesia on the radar screen of surf exploration.

boys wrap the nuts in leaves, place the resulting concoction in their mouths, and begin a slow mastication. Soon, they begin spitting red saliva into a plastic bucket, passed around as needed. "Want shum?" one asks, offering me the baggie of nuts. The prospect of returning to the plane, my mouth and lips red with evidence of my airport misadventure, at first deters me.

"I don't accept candy from strangers," I tell them gravely.

"What candy?" asks the boy holding the plastic baggie. "This betel!"

"Well, I don't accept betel, either," I amend.

"We not strangers," a buck-toothed boy puts in. "We all neighbors."

"Yeah, we all from same village," the AC-DC fan asserts. "You da stranger!"

Satisfied with their rebuttal to my concerns, the boys grin at me like crimson-toothed Cheshire Cats.

"You got me there," I admit.

I succumb to the betel-chewers' logic and examine the proffered baggie. The nuts look innocuous enough, and after I crack one open with my teeth, spread the crystalline condiment upon the yellowish insides, and wrap it (as instructed) in one of the leaves, I briefly envision the curiosity as an exotic confection. Once chewed, however, the leaf-wrapped nut transforms into a grainy mash that sucks the saliva from my mouth. A tingle spreads across my tongue, leaving bitterness in its wake. For braving such unpleasantry, I get rewarded with a slight dizziness and a burning sensation in my cheeks. With declining enthusiasm, I chew the betel for another minute, and then expunge the mash into the plastic bucket.

"You not like it, meeshter?" the boys ask.

"The flavor could use some more R&D," I reply, mustering a tone of diplomacy while I pick betel fibers from my teeth.

"R&D?" the buck-toothed boy asks, perplexed.

"Research and Development," I explain. The boys nod, though I can tell from their blank stares that the phrase has little meaning to them. Silence, punctuated by the occasional spit wad, descends on the gang. Seeing groups of passengers return to the plane, I bid the betel-chewers farewell and head across the tarmac, careful to keep a hand on my hat.

Back aboard the plane, I settle into my seat. The sun, declining through late afternoon, bathes the scene in a mellow light, dimmed now and again by scudding clouds. With a roar and a rush, the jet departs, but the "sleeping lady" slumbers on, her mountainous profile diminishing, as we gain altitude, to simply mountains. Cindy comes down the aisle and I order a beer, which I use to rinse my taste buds of the alkaline betel aftertaste.

The announcement for our arrival in Pohnpei comes as the last sliver of sun clings to the horizon. A high island, its lagoon home to smaller islets, its terrain blurred in the deepening twilight, comes into view. Clustered lights, the electric signature of the main town, Kolonia, guide our landing approach. The airport, situated on a lagoon islet connected by a causeway to the town, greets us with a squall that splatters thick raindrops on the windows. We taxi toward a cement building, its blue fluorescent lights magnets for swarms of moths. There, with about a dozen other passengers, I step out into the rain, my mind in a stupor of sleep deprivation, alcohol, and poorly-digested airplane cuisine. Beyond the immigration desk, palm fronds chatter in the darkness.

Excerpt from a Diary, August 1999:

Cradled in its mother's arms, the child stares at me, its eyes like two pools of chocolate frosted by the blue glow of fluorescent lights. Self-conscious, I wonder how many other pairs of eyes also hold me in their gaze, curious about the tall American wearing jeans and leather shoes in the sweat-inducing tropical night. I make a pretense of inspecting my baggage claim stubs and reading the fine print on my passport. Meanwhile, sandwiched in line between the staring child and an old woman who smells of stale perfume, I inch toward the immigration desk.

Across the room, a ceiling fan squeaks and wobbles, exhausted from its efforts to circulate the air.

The child, groping a hand toward a moth, briefly averts its gaze. The moth flutters away, and the pools of chocolate regard me once again. This time I smile a silent "hello." The child hides behind its mother's arm, which, like a brown pillow, offers ample padding for concealment.

The squeak of the ceiling fan grows more insistent. As it wobbles on its mounting, I wonder if the fan circulates the air, or rather, the air circulates the fan.

Playing peek-a-boo, the child pokes its head out. Warming to the game, I close my eyes, and then flash a face like a roaring lion — eyes wide, tongue out, and mouth agape. In response, the child bursts into tears, cheeks flushing a deeper shade of red with each successive wail. Seeking the source of her child's displeasure, the mother turns around, and heeding some sense of protective intuition, directs an accusatory glance at me.

"Pweirengid," she mutters, dark brows bristling.

The people in line laugh as the syllables of the strange word echo in my ears.

Later, I find the word in the glossary of my guidebook. "Pweirengid," it lists. English translation: "Idiot."

Chapter 2: Visions from Another Time

The immigration officer, his pudgy cheeks drooping over the collar of his uniform, scrutinizes me through narrow eyes that see something villainous in my visage. In broken English, he informs me that my one-way ticket raises suspicion. *Don't I have proof of onward travel?* I produce instead my teaching contract and place it on the counter like a gambler presenting a winning card.

The officer makes a show of document inspection, occasionally hovering his finger over certain passages, as though troubled by questionable verbiage.

As I await judgment, a voice calls out from the crowd beyond the immigration desk. "It's O.K., Wonpat. He's with the college." Jasper Orr, whose Midwestern drawl I remember from my phone interview with the COM Lang/Lit faculty, waves a greeting. His countenance, of a blue-eyed, blond bearded variety made particularly disarming by a wide flash of a smile, vouchsafes me a credibility that helps dispel the officer's doubts. As suspicion grudgingly gives way to assistance, the officer stamps my passport and scribbles some notations on a square of blue cardstock.

"Bring card to Department of Justice for work permit," the officer instructs.

My documents in order, Jasper helps with my luggage. In addition to my duffel bag, my gear, piled unceremoniously with the baggage of other passengers, now includes a large suitcase and a padded surfboard bag. Beyond the terminal, cars and taxis await along a gravel roadside. As my eyes adjust to the night, I notice Jasper study his car and frown. Surfboards and Japanese subcompacts, I infer, make for an uncomfortable combination.

"Uh, I should inform you," he says, searching for a delicate way to convey bad news, "there aren't any beaches here."

I reply that my interest concerns waves breaking over reefs, or more particularly, reef passes, of which the island has several. Jasper raises his eyebrows, seemingly in appreciation of a new concept. The information helps explain the presence of a surfboard among my luggage but does little to enhance the cargo capacity of the car. Finally, I suggest a rudimentary solution. Opening my suitcase, I rummage for the roll of duct tape (useful for surfboard repairs) that I've packed along. Placing the board bag on top of the car, I unroll the tape as a surrogate rope, loop it over the bothersome baggage, through the windows and the roof's underside, then back.

"This should work, as long as we drive slowly," I suggest.

"No problem," Jasper says. "On Pohnpei, there's no other way to drive."

We meander at about fifteen miles per hour toward Kolonia. While Jasper concentrates on the circle of road illuminated by our headlights, I fight off my jet lag. Every now and then the curtains of roadside foliage draw apart, revealing cinder block homes with starkly lit windows, backlighting small groups of islanders who sit on porch steps or lean in doorways. Furtive dogs, their eyes reflecting the glare of our headlights, slink behind weeds and oil drums. The road curves, and I notice the gravel shoulder beside us slope off into pools of still water, home to glossy-leafed bushes with short spiky roots. A brackish air enters my nostrils.

"Mangrove swamp," Jasper explains, seeing me sniff the air. "It surrounds the whole island. But we're getting close to town. The docks and harbor lie just ahead."

Buildings begin to gather along the roadside. Streetlights appear, holding umbrellas of wan illumination over cement and glass storefronts, their commercial purpose indicated by faded signs. We curve onto a long street where several cars, mostly representing the same genus and species as Jasper's sedan, plod through town with mollusk-minded ambition.

"I appreciate the ride," I remark, as we inch along. "I hope it's not too much trouble."

"No trouble at all," Jasper says. "In case you didn't know, we're neighbors. The College Personnel Office arranged housing for you in the apartment next to mine. Mayra Linskey, one of our department colleagues, lives just up the hill. In the evening we often sit on her front step, have a few drinks, and enjoy the view."

We roll past a few more storefronts and follow a side road

away from town. The streetlights disappear, and the smell of mangrove swamp returns. Spanning a black tongue of still water, a bridge brings us to "Rayleen Store." Situated on the front lawn of a house, the "store" consists of a shipping container with a window counter cut in one side. The glow of a Coleman lantern reveals a few women peering out from behind the counter, a limited inventory of toilet paper and Spam arranged on shelves behind them. As we pass, the women wave, and Jasper slows, turning on to a dirt track just opposite the store. We jostle up a steep hill, reach a level grassy space, and beam our headlights upon a long, peak-roofed wooden building, its back wall nestled against the hillside.

"Welcome to Fern Cove," Jasper says. "You have the second door, near the far end."

Lights from Jasper's porch provide illumination as we lug my gear across the grass to my apartment.

"Look out for dog-doo," Jasper advises. "Mayra's dog, Chips, likes to roam here."

I register the warning but leave my steps to fate as waves of fatigue make carrying even my suitcase a struggle. The desire to stretch out and have a real sleep, held in check through my journey, now increases with my proximity to a real bed. I drag my bags in and give the quarters a brief survey. A vinyl couch, T.V., wooden table with chairs, and refrigerator provide a semi-furnished comfort. A small hall leads to a bathroom. Midway down the hall, a door opens to a bedroom and the furnishing that, at present, I care about most: a bed. The sight brings forth a series of yawns.

Opening the fridge, Jasper reveals that he and Mayra supplied me with a care package: a jar of peanut butter, a box of wheat crackers, and a can of mixed nuts, augmented by two six-packs of Australian beer.

Fern Cove bungalow. The landholding families of Kolonia based rent not on market value but on the well-known fact that the college paid faculty a 600-dollar housing stipend. Whether faculty lived in a jungle shack, a hillside house, or a waterfront manor, the monthly rent matched what the college paid.

"We thought you'd feel more welcome if you arrived to find something in your fridge," Jasper informs me. "Tomorrow you should go up to the college, so you can get acquainted with the facilities and staff and arrange your office. If I'm too busy, maybe the Linskeys can give you a ride in the morning," Jasper plans, checking his watch. He leaves the apartment key on the kitchen table and departs. I lock the door, turn off the light, and sprawl on the mattress.

With a din capable of awakening Kosrae's sleeping lady, a rooster army signals the arrival of morning. Satisfied with the disruption of my sleep, the cries gradually desist, until only a few random bursts sound in the distance. Yellow rays filter through my window blinds, revealing my abode in greater detail: linoleum tile, peeling from the underlying cement slab; a wall poster, depicting rainforest birds of Micronesia; a gecko, eyeing me stoically while clinging upside down to the ceiling. Curious about the world beyond my wall, I open the blinds to what looks like a vision from another time. A mirror-surfaced bay, tinted gold in the light of the swift-rising sun, gleams amid a semi-circle of rainforest slopes. At intervals, the slopes' rainforest canopy gives way to silver waterfalls. Winged forms swoop from the heights, glide along the bay, and fade to specks among the trees of the far shore. Along the water's edge, wisps of mist rise and curl in a dance of water spirits.

Welcome to Fern Cove, I muse, recalling Jasper's words from the previous night. The beauty of the morning helps me forget my complaint against the roosters and lures me to poke my head outside the window sill, which lies partially shaded by a stand of papaya trees. One papaya tree plays host to group of orange-beaked birds, who gorge on the tree's dangled fruits. The birds glance at me to assess what competition I might pose to their breakfast plans. Meanwhile, a sweet fragrance tickles my nose, drawing my attention to a stand of flowering shrubs, their bright

Fern Cove, August 1999. Daily vistas such as this made for a perk not listed in my teaching contract but very much appreciated. As for the papayas dangling in the foreground—birds usually got to them before I could, pecking large holes into the rinds just as the fruit reached marginal ripeness.

blooms a colorful salutation to the morning. *What do you seek, traveler?* the flowers seem to query. *You who wear the residue of car exhaust and city dust—do you wish our fragrance to clear your mind? Linger, then, and clear your mind. Contemplate this outdoor room, where an exuberance of plumeria bloom.* Taken by the surrounding beauty, I let a blanket of relaxation pass over me, and resolve to wash away the grime of travel with a cool shower.

A half hour later, refreshed and enjoying a breakfast of crackers smeared with peanut butter, I hear a knock on my door. Expecting Jasper, or perhaps the Linskeys, I open the door, only to find a lithe blonde woman barefoot on the porch, a Ziploc bag of brownies in her hands. As best I can with peanut butter stuck to the roof of my mouth, I bid the stranger hello.

"G'day!" she says, her Australian accent dramatizing the greeting. "I'm Lana, one of the Australian Volunteers. I just baked these fresh and decided to donate the batch to my neighbors. You must be the new English teacher!" Around her lips, a few brown crumbs testify to her own sampling of the wares.

I accept the brownies, and seeing beads of perspiration on her forehead, invite Lana to step in out of the rapidly warming morning.

"Oh, no worries," she says. "I live a short walk from here, just past Rayleen store. Anyway, things will cool off soon. Rain's coming."

I scan the sky, but see only a few puffy clouds, impossibly distant, offering little hint of shade, let alone a portent of precipitation.

"I get my information from the wind, not the sky," the lithe lady explains, sensing my lack of faith in her weather forecast. Giggling, she looks at her feet. Her toenails each sport a carefully painted smiley face. "Well, don't you wish to try a brownie?" she asks, wiggling her toes so the smiley faces appear to laugh.

"I dunno," I say, my tongue fumbling through an adhesive coating of peanut butter. "I just had breakfast. Maybe I'll set them aside as a mid-day snack."

"Suit yourself. I think this batch might be a little more. . . *potent* than usual . . . enjoy!" She walks off, and in response to my word of thanks, replies that she just likes to do her part for international relations.

As the morning progresses, the temperature increase raises rivulets of sweat on my chest, and my shirt clings to my skin like a wet towel. I sprawl on the couch and pant. Through their Ziploc bag, Lana's brownies waft a sweet aroma through my abode, luring me for a sample. Somehow the effort required to walk to the counter and put a brownie in my mouth seems like a Herculean task amid heat that makes even breathing a chore. *Brownies?* I mutter. *I wish Lana had brought me an electric fan!* Eventually, seduced by the aroma, I overcome my lethargy, muddle to the counter, and take a brownie from the bag. Nibbling off a corner, I enjoy a burst of fudge, moist yet hearty, inspiration for more enthusiastic chomping. Only after I've devoured two brownies do I stop to ponder their peculiar aftertaste.

Before I can subject the brownies to further scrutiny, the clatter of a poorly-muffled engine and dysfunctional suspension sounds outside my door. I step outside to investigate, and see a grinning couple beckon me aboard a junkyard-issue specimen of island transportation. Its body an assortment of scavenged parts, the jeep resembles an art project more than a practical vehicle. "Hi Jacques! Welcome to Pohnpei," the woman greets me, raising her voice above the din of the engine. "I'm Mayra Linskey, and this is my husband Todd."

Wearing a loose-fitting floral print dress and sandals, Mayra looks casually in tune with the climate, yet manages to exude a seriousness of purpose, and looks at her watch as if to verify our compliance with some schedule. "Jasper thought we should let you sleep in after your flight," she says, "but we better get up to the college now to get your paperwork started." Todd turns the Jeep around and we clatter down the hillside track.

"Great to meet you, Mayra," I say. "I remember your voice from my phone interview; it's nice to finally match it with a face." Turning to Todd, I offer my appreciation for the ride. "Nice Jeep you have here."

"It's a work in progress," Todd says, grinding the gears as we transition to the paved road.

"It must be the envy of the island," I reply, in polite recognition of the obvious effort required to customize the vehicle.

"Yeah, when it's not broken down," Mayra confides, looking at her husband in the manner of one expressing a grievance. The engine quiets as it settles into gear.

"It should get us to the college at least," Todd states hopefully.

We drive over the bridge, and I discover a view of Fern Cove invisible the night before. The bay, I observe, represents an inland-thrust of the wide lagoon that surrounds the island. Looking seaward, I see the lagoon's depth indicated by changes in color, with brushstrokes of aquamarine near the shallows, and swaths of cyan in the deeper regions. At the far edge of this palette, flecks of white surf, and cobalt blue beyond, mark the border between the island's barrier reef and the open Pacific. Once over the bridge, we lose the vista to mangroves crowded thick by the roadside.

Several minutes later, joining a procession of Tokyo metal in which the Jeep provides an odd bit of Americana, we crawl forward at a pace that mocks our desire for a cool breeze. A crate-laden truck burps black exhaust, wrapping my head in a suffocating blanket of diesel. My ears boom to the sound of my pulse. I grow dizzy, while my mouth turns suddenly dry, as if a wad of cotton absorbed the saliva. Trying not to obsess about my list of discomforts, I focus on Kolonia's hodge-podge sights. A café, serving a lonely patron, wafts a spiral of fish-smelling smoke into the air. Retail shops juxtapose incongruously with a monolithic cement building (the telecom center, Todd informs me) whose roof bristles with antennas and satellite dishes. Inside the post office, a postal clerk rests his elbows on the counter and

FSM Post Office, Ponape (note the old-style spelling, a legacy of the Trust Territory era). The U.S. zip code did little to expedite delivery. Mail often spent two weeks in transit and an additional week languishing behind the counter.

stares back through the entry doors at the passersby. Dominating the skyline, the awesome basalt promontory of Sokeh's Rock stands sentinel, guarding some hidden mystery. Based on my impressions of a night and a morning, Kolonia fits the profile of a typical Pacific backwater: lazy commerce, lethargic traffic, and rusting corrugated roofs.

Unlike its backwater brethren, the supermarket, with a shiny modern storefront, hosts a bustle of activity. Swerving into the parking lot, Todd finds a parking space in the semi-shade of the market's side wall, and to my relief, suggests we procure refreshments. Todd and Mayra bound out of the Jeep, eager for air-conditioned aisles stocked with cold beverages. Of similar inclination, I move to follow, only to discover my feet hang like lead weights on the end of rubber band legs. I take a step, falter, and rest my arm against the Jeep for support.

"Aren't you coming, Jacques?" Mayra asks.

"You go on ahead. I'll catch up," I say. What comes out of my mouth sounds more like *"You iguana, I'm ketchup."*

Intrigued by my puzzling pronunciation, Mayra peers at me intently. "You feel O.K.?" she asks, full of motherly concern. "Maybe you should just stay here and rest in the shade."

Todd approaches and asks Mayra about the trouble.

"He must really have some jet lag," Mayra says. "His eyes look so. . .*red*."

Todd scrutinizes me. With his forefinger, he traces a circle through the air in front of my nose. In the wake of the finger, I see an animated trail form, hang suspended before my face, and then drift away like a smoke ring.

Sheesh. What did Lana put in those brownies?

"Jet lag, eh?" Todd remarks with a wry grin. He turns and follows Mayra into the market.

In a certain subset of the population—a subset to which I belong—the "high" produced by psychotropic drugs brings not

34

giddy joy, nor deep philosophical insight, but rather sheer terror. Accordingly, while the small portion of my brain capable of rational thought chastises me for eating *two* brownies brought to my door by a stranger whose psychological stability and culinary competence I accepted on faith, the rest of me succumbs to dark visions.

Into the kettle drum resonance of my pulse comes the thud of a bouncing basketball. Baggy-shorted boys, shuffling through the parking lot, jostle each other for the ball, and knock it accidentally in my direction. They give chase, only to swerve abruptly when they see an elderly man hobble toward the car parked in the space alongside the Jeep. As the man comes close I see the reason for his troubled gait. His left foot, wrapped partially in a white cloth, resembles a swollen stump. Obscuring his toes, grainy scales intermix with ulcerated purple flesh. The three smallest toes seem eaten away, or else hidden under the swollen mass.

"Leper! Leper!" the kids shout, steering clear of him.

Stoically, the man puts his groceries in the car, haltingly positions himself in the driver's seat, and meets my gaze with the pained expression of those resigned to suffering without hope. Shuddering, I recall one of my guidebook's unpleasant factoids: though rare, leprosy remains a stubborn illness in parts of the Pacific.

Amid such thoughts, the Linskeys return with a four-pack of Starbucks Frappuccinos. "These should help the drive pass more easily," Mayra says, with a hopeful tone that reveals a complete ignorance of my condition.

Under the influence of Lana's brownies, I watch the Jeep progress through a strange terrain, into which my paranoia injects a strain of Frappuccino-resistant fear. When we summit the slopes above Kolonia and glimpse a vista of the town and harbor, where buildings, boats, and lagoon islets resemble miniatures in a model-maker's diorama, I picture us crashing through the guardrail and plunging off the precipice. As we traverse a valley of ramshackle homes, where dogs and pigs roll in the dirt of wire-fenced yards, I envision packs of predators, hungry for the taste of English teacher. In the silver pools of a rainforest creek, where women wash clothes and brown children swim naked, I imagine a parasitic pestilence. Inevitably, my morbid mindset manifests a physical reaction: a growing nausea that I endure with clenched teeth. I know I'm going to barf, and probably all over the back seat of the Jeep, unless we arrive at the college past-haste.

We pass a small volcanic spire, lumped on the plain like a pile of petrified poo (Chickenshit Mountain, Todd announces), its tortured topography a metaphor of my own inner upheaval. The road bends away from the oddly-named landmark, cuts a swath through more sugarcane, and approaches a group of two-storey buildings, their white cement walls stark against the green fields and blue horizon beyond. Todd, swerving abruptly into a gravel parking lot, nearly turns my stomach inside out. With clenched teeth, I resist regurgitation.

"Well, Jacques, here it is—the COM-FSM campus," Mayra announces, hopping out of the Jeep. "Todd thinks it looks more like a high school than a college, but at least it pays our bills! First, we'll introduce you to some colleagues, and then we'll go see Teana, the Language Division secretary. She can provide your office and classroom keys."

"B-b-bathroom," I stammer. "Gotta find a bathroom!"

"Oh, of course. . ." Mayra intones. She gestures vaguely toward a door in a building across the lawn. "Over there."

Perhaps thinking the location of the bathroom self-evident, Todd and Mayra leave me to my own devices, and exchange greetings with several students propped on a nearby wall. After lurching through waves of nausea, I arrive at the indicated area, only to discover a maintenance closet. Doggedly,

The volcanic spire known as Chickenshit Mountain, part of the King-Kong landscape that infused an element of the exotic into my daily commute.

I follow a path along the building's perimeter, around a corner, and, to my frustration, into a small secluded parking lot. Other than an electric maintenance cart and a few parked cars, the area appears deserted. When another wave of nausea doubles me over, I surrender at last, hurling the contents of my stomach upon the pavement. Up comes a mocha magma, smelling sweetly of Frappuccino, followed by a fusillade of fudge, as successive heaves summon remnants of brownie. *So much for international relations,* I think, cursing Lana and her curious confections.

A final dry heave leaves me in that enervated, post-purge state characterized by a burning esophagus and throbbing temples. Gradually, I recover my wits, and register details overlooked during my emetic emergency. For one, the parking spot now covered with the former contents of my stomach belongs, according to a sign, to the college's Vice President of Instruction. For another, I realize that one of the parked cars contains an occupant: a heavy-set woman whose brows bristle under a helmet of frizzy raven hair. Her expression conveys such opprobrium that I feel responsible for an act of extreme depravity. Unsure of the proper etiquette for such situations, I give her a sheepish grin, and slink away to rejoin Todd and Mayra.

I find them engaged in conversation with a guitar-toting girl whose T-shirt spells "Chuukita" in bold pink letters. After a bit of thought, I decipher the wordplay, which combines Chuuk (a.k.a. Truk), an island group to the west, and "Chiquita," Spanish for "girl." Interpreting my deduction as a sign of renewed cognitive competence, I interject myself into the conversation. "Chuukita!" I blurt, pointing to the shirt. "Girl from Chuuk!"

The girl blinks in surprise. "Ya, I from Chuuk," she says. "My uncle gave me shirt. You like it?" she asks, posing coquettishly.

"Renleen, this is Jacques, our new English teacher," Mayra says, interceding. "He traveled all the way from

California, so he's still a bit loopy." Placing a concerned hand on my shoulder, Mayra asks if I feel better after my visit to the bathroom.

"Better," I reply, ignoring the part about the bathroom.

"I still see some jet lag in your eyes," Mayra says. "Let's visit the Language Arts Office. I'll find some coffee and cookies to perk you up."

Mayra leads me past a row of tinted windows, through a door, and into a room of cubicles made wintry by air conditioning and the white glow of fluorescent lights. The sudden chill raises goose bumps on my arms. Meanwhile, the room's occupants, to whom Mayra introduces me as "the new English teacher," crowd me with curiosity. Accompanied by the universal cuisine of academia—coffee and cookies—I make my acquaintance with a sample of my Language Arts colleagues. Like Mayra, they express a seriousness of purpose regarding their educational mission, yet put me at ease with their casual demeanor, projecting nothing of the intellectual smugness that seasoned faculty sometimes use to supercilious effect on new hires.

Fred Knox, a barrel-chested man with wire-rimmed spectacles and a touch of gray upon his temples, speaks in humble tones when he describes how he left a successful business career for "service to the deprived youth of the world." A missionary educator, he recalls visiting Africa and Asia before settling in Micronesia. One of the college's original faculty members, he sees teaching as a spiritual duty, and supplements his college load by working afternoons at a small village high school on the island's east side. "You'll only survive out here if you see this job as a calling," he says, peering at me through spectacles apparently calibrated to provide a measure of my teaching commitment.

"Fred gave me the same lecture when I first arrived," Mayra says. "For all his talk about commitment, you'd think he could commit to making a decent pot of coffee. This one tastes

COM-FSM National Campus, circa 1999. Tradewinds, gusting through open windows, provided a natural climate-control for classrooms. A student body of approximately 750 full-time students, served by 40 faculty (mostly from the U.S. and Canada), enrolled in programs that included Liberal Arts, Accounting, Agriculture, Business, Marine Science, Pre-nursing, and Teacher Education. Students wishing to pursue their studies beyond the AA/AS degree typically transferred to Guam and Hawaii. Those transferring to the U.S. mainland expressed a preference for the University of Oregon, which maintained an admissions program for Pacific islanders.

like old socks!"

Katy Jones, a petite brunette in her late thirties, seems well-inured to Fred's coffee, filling the pauses in conversation with eager sips from her mug. Hired on a Title 3 Grant to help develop the College's distance education infrastructure, Katy spends her workday by a computer screen. Her job lasts as long as the grant money does, after which she'll return to "the good ole' USA." Meanwhile, in her spare time, she indulges a habit of fiction reading. "Did you bring out any recent bestsellers?" she asks me, a hopeful look in her brown eyes.

"What she'd really like is a good romance novel," Mayra clarifies. "Preferably one brimming with the amorous adventures of the tall, dark, and handsome."

"After a day in front of my computer, I'd settle for kinda tall, a touch of gray, and aging gracefully," Katy says, generating a round of laughs.

Amiko, a young Japanese woman who averts her eyes as I go to shake her hand, occupies a desk situated in the back corner of the room. Apart from a wall poster depicting Mt. Fuji, her Spartan cubicle contains little décor; a notepad, a jar of pens, and a desk calendar sit in precise arrangement. "I here with JOCV," Amiko tells me in a mouse-like voice.

"J-O-what?" I inquire

"Japanese Overseas Cooperation Volunteers," Mayra clarifies, when Amiko has difficulty pronouncing the phrase. "Each semester, the College schedules a few Japanese language classes, which Amiko teaches. Though we give Amiko office space, she's not officially an employee of the College, but rather the JOCV, the Japanese version of the Peace Corps." Amiko smiles shyly upon hearing her job description.

"You'll probably meet the rest of the Language Arts faculty over the next few days," Mayra says. "Now let's go visit Teana, the Division secretary."

41

We go back outside and pause before the door of an adjacent office. Mayra places her hand on the knob but hesitates before opening the door.

"The faculty here are an easy-going group, and generally get along" she confides in low tones. "However, you should be careful around Teana. She has connections all over the island. If you stay on her good side, life becomes much easier. Need an apartment? Ask Teana. Need a car? Ask Teana. Need a wife. . ."

"Ask Teana?" I infer.

Mayra nods. "Try not to forget her when her birthday rolls around," she says, finally opening the door.

I prepare a smile full of charm, but it turns to an embarrassed grimace. Before me, administering a desk covered in notes and scattered papers, she sits, the bushy-browed woman who saw me puke in the parking lot. Unimpressed by my professorial pretense, she surveys my countenance, and as the corners of her mouth slant into a scowl, I sense the rebuke of a staff member who perceives the buffoon at my troglodytic core.

"Hi Teana," Mayra says. "Meet Jacques, our new English teacher!"

Excerpt from a Diary, August 1999:

I exist in a state of sensory overload, where the familiar attributes of the world seem re-packaged, infused with a surreal intensity. In the East, the dawn detonates, filling the sky with a lavish light, to which hillsides rise resplendent, sparking hibiscus red and plumeria white. Across the valley, waterfalls turn to threads of molten silver, dangling from obsidian heights. The bay beneath Fern Cove begins to glow, its surface an incandescence that rasps the retina.

Then, just as the radiance turns repressive, a cloud intervenes, dimming the sun, tracing a shadow like a soothing balm upon the landscape. More follow, spreading gray where once the sun held sway. A breath of damp air disrupts the heat and brings a scent of the rainforest. Soon, there comes a sound of rain, like a nymph pattering among jungle leaves. Suddenly, a cloud tears its belly on the trees of my front yard, and a torrent ensues. The collective evaporation of the tropical Pacific targets my roof, impacting in an aqueous explosion. As a waterfall cascades off the awning, I think that gravity alone couldn't account for the velocity of the rain; rather, the rain, like the sun, has a will, primal and mysterious. I listen, transfixed, until I hear in splashing rivulets an echo of ancient seas hissing upon a lava-laden shore, and envision in falling silver drops a remnant of the light that shone when the moon was still young, and feathers were only a dream to the ancestors of birds.

Chapter 3: A Parliament of Expats

Gavin Grier, a hospitality management consultant and part-time instructor at the College, sports the sunburned face and scruffy beard of a man just returned from long outdoor adventure. Wanting an audience for his tale, Gavin disturbs the tranquility of a Fern Cove afternoon, honking the horn of his car, a rattletrap sedan from which he produces a grocery bag containing several bottles of Australian wine. The alcohol lures Mayra, Jasper and I all too easily from planning our syllabi for the upcoming semester. Joined by Todd, we sit on the Linskey's porch and watch the sun progress to evening. When our conversation falters, we find amusement in the antics of the Linskey's dog, Chips, who chases birds, rolls on the grass, and whines for belly scratches from each of us.

Mayra, watching Gavin fill my glass, warns me to keep my guard up against his wicked influence. Noting my preference for carousal instead of curriculum, Gavin retorts that he simply helps others express their latent tendencies. With a gravitas rendered humorous by his disarming grin and the shock of copper hair which spikes from his scalp, Gavin announces that he didn't visit to discuss the quality of his character, but to report the results of his lifestyle experiment. Glasses in hand, we soon sit in rapt attention as Gavin divulges the details of the "Sandals Project," a two-month, island-hopping odyssey during which he carried nothing but the clothes on his back and a suitcase of cheap rubber flip-flops to barter for accommodation, food, and transport. The threads of narrative weave in my mind a tapestry of Robinson Crusoe escapades, set amid atolls whose names provide a tongue-twisting interplay of consonants and vowels: Pingelap, Mwoakilloa, Kapingamarangi. From an island where a dozen sandals procured a continuous supply of palm sap liquor, to a blue lagoon where dinner swam a spear-thrust away, the tale takes us to a region of the Pacific outside the scope of time. With a dreamy gaze that looks past us toward far-flung atolls beyond the horizon, Gavin informs us that "places still exist where one can go totally off the grid and still get by."

"Sounds like fun," Todd chimes in enthusiastically.

"In some ways," Gavin affirms. "Trading sandals for accommodation? No problem. Thanks to the continued migration of locals away from the atolls to the main islands, atoll villages have fish, coconuts, and houses to spare. Trading sandals for transport? Not so easy. When I tried to barter for my return passage, the captain of the *Caroline Voyager* said he didn't want my cheap trinkets and accused me of acting like a white colonist."

"White colonist, eh," Jasper remarks, eyeing Gavin's sunburn. "I'd say 'red colonist' would be more accurate."

Todd, eager for more details, probes further. "So, if the captain didn't want sandals, how did you get on board? You must have won him over somehow."

"I gave him my watch," Gavin says, holding up his wrist, where a white band of non-sunburned skin testifies to the former timepiece.

"You mean that fake Rolex you got in Saipan last year?" Jasper asks.

"The very one," Gavin chuckles.

"Talk about cheap trinkets!" Todd exclaims. "With all the junk I have, Mayra and I could barter our way to Australia."

"Great idea," Mayra says, her monotone clearly facetious.

A breeze, brushing our cheeks with a balmy hint of tropical seas, swirls the air, while a discovery of ripe fruit inspires several Lorikeets to add their screeches to the gossip of the rainforest. Reflections and shadows spread around fishermen paddling a lone canoe upon the waters below Fern Cove. *Off the grid*, I think to myself. The phrase carries a metaphor applicable to the scene before me. Gathering crustaceans from the shallows, the fishermen, perhaps a father and son, reproduce a scene from the ancients.

We sip our wine and watch Chips dig among the betel trees that mark the perimeter of the lawn. Compared to the mongrel strays known to frequent the trash heaps of Kolonia, the

Betel tree (properly known as the Areca Palm). An islander's betel bravado was often indicated by the degree to which the chewing habit—particularly, the habit of mixing lime powder with the nuts—resulted in tooth erosion. Landholding families cultivated betel for personal enjoyment, use as a folk medicine, and for its barter value in the underground economy

dog, with muscular haunches and a shiny coat, could model the well-loved American pet from a Norman Rockwell painting.

"Good-looking dog," I remark casually.

"The locals probably think so too," Gavin states. "They probably can't wait to make a meal of his tasty hindquarters."

"Gavin!" Mayra scolds indignantly. "How could you think such a thing?"

"And, how could he know which parts of a dog qualify as tasty?" Jasper probes. "I wonder if Gavin has something further to share about his atoll adventure."

The red of embarrassment enhances the sunburn on Gavin's face. With a grin, Gavin confesses that one who roams far upon the Fringe must eventually sample its cuisine. Watching our initial disgust give way to curiosity, Gavin briefly recounts his dog-meat dinner, which, he informs us, had a texture and taste like pot roast. Meanwhile, happily unaware of our conversation, Chips returns tail-a-wag to Mayra, who shoos him and his hindquarters inside.

"Post roast," Todd intones, half to himself. "I'd give an arm and a leg for a real pot roast, stewed with fresh carrots and potatoes, like we used to cook back in the States."

"Oh, no kidding!" Mayra concurs. "As for me, I could use a slice of New York cheesecake for dessert."

"Or a bottle of sherry, and some good cigars," Gavin adds.

"Don't indulge in thoughts like that," Jasper warns.

The mention of fantasy food makes Todd and Mayra stare at their feet despondently.

"I don't think I've seen a bottle of sherry or a cigar since we've been on this island," Todd ponders.

"I don't think I've seen a slice of cheesecake since we lived in the U.S.," Mayra adds.

For a while, my companions brood in silence, dreaming

49

of distant desserts. Perhaps eager to change the mood, Gavin changes the subject, and inquires how I like my ex-pat life. With an air of professionalism intended to impress my new colleagues, I affirm my eagerness to begin teaching duties at the modern and well-equipped main campus.

"Forget the campus," Gavin says. "How do you like the three W's?"

"The three W's?" I inquire.

"Most ex-pats," Gavin explains, "come out for the job, but stay for the three W's: wine, women, and wandering."

I reply that other than the wine just consumed, I've mostly indulged in beer.

"Not a bad start," Gavin says.

"Come on, Gavin," Mayra chides. "Not everyone fits under your ex-pat classifications. Some of us actually care about work."

Mayra looks to Jasper for support, but Jasper shrugs and brings his glass to his lips. "I don't think work counts as one of the three W's," he says. "At least not as Gavin defines them."

"I care about *my* work," Todd offers optimistically.

Mayra surveys the detritus of half-completed art projects scattered around the lawn and frowns in the manner of a woman who endures rather than enjoys her husband's hobbies.

Gavin finishes his wine and stands. "Now that we've had our appetizers, anyone care to join me for the main course?"

"Uh-oh," Mayra sighs.

"Let me guess: Rumours Bar?" Jasper speculates.

"Actually, Club Cupid," Gavin says. "The Peace Corps is having a party."

"Now doesn't that seem appropriate?" Mayra says, more as a statement than a question.

"A Peace Corps party?" Todd asks.

"No. That Gavin just returned from two months of island

50

hopping, and already knows where the party is."

Prodded by our party provocateur, we find the path of least resistance leads not back to lesson-planning but to Club Cupid. We pile in to the Sheldon's jeep, jostle down the hillside path, and accelerate along the waterfront road. Evening air, slightly cooler and redolent of rainforest blossoms, swirls about us. Near Club Cupid—a bar perched on a mountaintop behind Kolonia—the scenery grows increasingly cinematic. The last sunrays—shafts of orange light that spear through ferns and palms—give a pink airbrush to clouds that scud seemingly just overhead. Todd downshifts when the last hundred yards of road morph into a steep dirt track. We bounce up to a gravel-and-grass plateau with a dual function of bar parking lot and vista point, where Seekers of the Sunset, holding cameras or special companions, look west in supplication. Magnetized by the vista, I jump from the Jeep and walk toward the crowd, until Gavin mentions we can see just as well from inside. "We'll want to order drinks before the sunset crowd does," he points out in a tone that suggests his prior experience in the matter.

Based on the chatter that greets our ears, the club already hosts a lively mob. Sunset hues, entering through floor-to-ceiling windows, paint a fiery glow upon the walls. A waitress, whose make-up looks applied with a paintbrush, takes Gavin's order for a round of beers. Meanwhile I scan the room. A bald man, meaty tattooed arms burgeoning from a tank top, sits at the bar, his hand placed possessively upon the exposed waistline of an island girl whose bare midriff and too-tight shorts draw the gaze of several patrons. The girl giggles as the man instructs her in the proper technique for bouncing a quarter into a shot glass. By the far wall, a pool table centers a crowd of young islanders and Americans, some wearing T-shirts emblazoned with the dove- star flag of the Peace Corps. An occasional hoot erupts from the crowd when one of them completes a difficult shot. In the middle of the room,

Club Cupid, at the intersection of pastel panorama and expat entertainment. Though travelers seeking a true immersion in Micronesian culture designated as "touristy" any drinking establishment other than a sakau bar, Club Cupid had a special allure, and, in conjunction with Club Flamingo (the largest bar in the FSM) and the Rumours Bar (a juke joint nestled among the harbor-front mangroves), functioned as a hotspot of Kolonia nightlife. Ironically, Saturday night revelry often gave way to Sunday sermons, as the vista point provided a meeting ground for a Filipino congregation of the Church of Christ.

seated or standing around tables, an assortment of expats and locals drink, chat, and survey the crowd, their brows furrowing in scrutiny of new faces or lifting in recognition of others. The waitress returns with our beers, and Gavin raises a toast to "life on the Fringe."

As the sunset fades, a neon Budweiser sign behind the bar flickers to life, while recessed ceiling lights glow dimly. A pair of teenage girls, their underage status raising little alarm, brushes past us on their way to the pool table. Gavin, following them with his gaze, draws Mayra's admonishment. "Now Gavin, even you have standards. Those girls could be in your class someday."

Gavin takes a long guzzle. "Wait until I get my beer goggles on," he says. "Then talk to me about my standards."

Perturbed by Gavin's reply, and perhaps additionally by the goofy grunts of laughter which it inspires, Mayra announces she's through with "guy talk. Waving to an acquaintance, a local lass attired in the island style of baggy blouse and skirt, she relocates to a domain of more demure discourse. Bereft of Mayra's tempering influence, we descend once again toward guy talk, alighting on subjects that befit our increasing inebriation. As Gavin offers his insights about Peace Corps girls and their potential for island romance, a thick-set middle-aged man, his hair swept back with a greasy pomade whose sheen mingles with the gleam of forehead perspiration, gives Gavin a slap on the shoulder. In an Australian accent, he asks about Gavin's travels.

"Rumor has it ya got drunk and washed off the deck of a freighter," the Australian says. "Nice to see ya back in one piece."

"Thanks," Gavin says, delivering a shoulder-slap in return. "I wouldn't put much trust in rumors."

"Good policy, Mate! Well, if ya feel like tellin' the true story, the lads and I have a table 'round the corner there." He points past the bar to a shadowed enclave where grizzled revelers quaff their liquor with the intemperance of sots at a bacchanal.

"Why doncha join us for a round or two?" he offers, sauntering off.

Jasper expresses little enthusiasm for what he calls the "Ex-pat Parliament," a term rich in a satirical irony meant to convey a low opinion of the parliament's members, but his misgivings get lost in the bibulous bravado that Gavin incites as he herds us toward the indicated table. Though we suspect that joining Barton and the lads means a second dose of Gavin's travel narrative, Todd and I make no objections.

Over the next hour, I glimpse how the pursuit of wine, women, and wandering guides the lives of various characters. Vick Burns, a traveling educator, displays a passion for intoxication that matches, if not exceeds, his interest in the subject of history. Hanley Ashe, publicly a collector of Pacific antiquities, less publicly collects romantic affairs during sojourns to various islands. Barry Enns, a former Peace Corps volunteer, works by day as a dive instructor and by night as a dispenser of advice about how to meet island women. These and others seek to outdo each other in listing their island exploits and vowing never to return to mainland life. Ever interested in new adventure, they applaud Gavin's "journey off the grid" and, seeking vicarious participation, offer suggestions for its improvement. One of the table's elder statesmen, whom the lads nickname "Tin Can" in honor of his service as a destroyer radar operator — a history commemorated by Tin Can's "USS Ingersoll DD990" baseball hat — opines that Spam, rather than money or sandals, serves as the best currency for Pacific travel.

"I haven't yet found an island where a few cans of Spam couldn't procure just about anything," he says.

Murmurs of agreement rise from the group. Then Barry, the dive instructor, mentions the inconvenient fact that a cargo of Spam sufficient to barter one's way around the Pacific would require not just a duffel bag but a barge.

"You can go off the grid right here," he advises. "Just get a dive mask and a spear and head to the lagoon. You'll catch fish to spare."

"Or get a machete and enter the bush," Hanley adds. "You'll find tropical fruit a-plenty, I reckon."

"Ah, but sooner or later yer gonna want a drink," Barton warns. "And when ya do, you'll find the rest of us here, enjoying the view."

"Hmm. Nice view," Vick adds, and we see he refers not to the tropical night, which nuzzles against the windows of the bar, but to a pair of Peace Corps girls, who nuzzle their hips against the edge of the pool table. The sight proves sufficiently distracting to shift the conversation topic, and the members of the Ex-pat Parliament now assert their qualifications as connoisseurs of women. Over the next several minutes, no female in the bar remains immune to scrutiny. The teenage girls receive special attention, though a few voices of dissent echo Mayra's earlier admonition. "Somewhere those girls have fathers," Tin Can points out. "We might even know their families. Think of your reputations, gentlemen."

"Destroying one's reputation is what makes island life so fun," Barton proclaims, with an assuredness that bolsters the others, who cheer their agreement. Some even propose a toast to "destroying one's reputation," and glasses clink around the table. Their devotion to debauchery thus affirmed, Barton orders another round. Unsure of my enthusiasm for such sentiments, I delay my nomination for membership in the Ex-pat Parliament. For a change of scenery, I head to the pool table, where I learn not everyone fits the profile of the Westerner whose mission to Micronesia centers on hedonism. Sally, a blond twenty-something who wears a Peace Corps T-shirt over a long skirt, expresses great conviction in her contribution to the island and its people. I ask about the details of her Peace Corps service.

"I teach the islanders how to brush their teeth," she says, her fist a simulation of toothbrush technique. "I specialize in proper form."

"No kidding?" I remark, amazed that the Peace Corps employs American youth as toothbrush ambassadors.

"It's, like, *so* cool, you know?" she elaborates. "I had no idea I could make such a difference. The Peace Corps really helped me find my niche." She pronounces "niche" like "snitch," shortening the vowel and adding a post-vocalic *t*.

"It's pronounced 'neesh,'" I correct, drawing out the vowel. "Like *'sheesh'*—but without a post-vocalic 't.'"

"What are you, some kind of English teacher?" she asks, her cheeks flushed red with equal parts embarrassment and indignation.

"As a matter of fact, yes," I say, and proffer a smile that goes unrequited. "However, the word 'niche' is of French origin."

Before I can elaborate on pronunciation pedigree, Sally brushes me aside and rejoins her friends. Undeterred, I edge close to the pool table, where the party atmosphere carries overtones of spectator sport, as onlookers watch a slinky brunette in her fifties sink one challenging shot after another. Wearing a low-cut blouse that opens to overly-tanned cleavage, she confidently leans into her final shot and knocks the 8-ball home with a double carom. In a raspy smoker's voice, she asks "who's the queen?"

"Colette's the queen!" her onlookers reply, while her defeated opponent rests his cue on the table and returns to the gallery previously-chastened challengers.

"Anybody else?" the brunette inquires, casually rubbing chalk on the end of her cue.

Seeing nobody immediately respond, I step forward.

As I rack the balls, the woman looks me over. "Where you been hiding, Honey?" she asks. "I thought I knew all the guys around here."

I introduce myself and explain I'd flown in just a few days before.

"Nice to meet you, Jacques," she says.

As the standing winner, Colette elects to break, and spears the cue ball in a freewheeling style that shows little regard for shot sequencing. The break fails to pocket any balls, but rather scatters them haphazardly, and based on the carom action, I recognize the pool table as one known in pool parlance as "wet," its cloth and cushions rendered sluggish by humidity. "So, Jacques," Colette says as I survey the table, "I guess you got tired of drinking with Barton and his gang?"

"I guess so," I say, surprised to find my prior whereabouts in the bar a matter of scrutiny. With a soft shot, I sink a striped ball into a corner pocket, get a lucky roll from the cue ball, and go on a two-ball run before a bad leave places me in a blockade of Colette's solids.

"So, does that mean you aren't interested in ruining your reputation?" she asks. With a crisp smack she sends a solid into a corner pocket.

The question carries overtones of innuendo, and I seek a suitably coy response. "Maybe not just yet," I say.

Collete knocks down another solid, and then unaccountably dogs an easy ¼ ball hit that results in a scratch to the middle pocket. "I see," she says. Retrieving the cue ball, she comes close, places it in my palm, and lets her finger linger on my hand. A smell of cigarettes permeates her breath and helps dispel a façade that had influenced my earlier perception. While glossed with a sultry allure in the dimly lighted bar, up close Collete's face displays the haggard sadness of a woman hopelessly clinging to the vestiges of lost youth.

"Well, you look like a guy who knows how to treat a lady right," she whispers, bringing her lips close to my ear. "Now, take your shot."

The sultry intimations act like pixie dust, and I proceed to run the table, sinking the remaining four stripes in succession. As I ponder how to best knock down the 8-ball, the on-lookers—including Sally, her face still smoldering with displeasure over my well-meant but apparently unappreciated pronunciation lecture—crowd close, curious if Colette's defeat might finally be at hand. Colette, showing little apprehension, casually chalks her cue, and sidles to the end rail opposite me, her cleavage placed in my line of sight. She gives me a wink.

"8-ball, far corner," I announce, calling the shot per standard billiard protocol. Feeling the eyes of the spectators, I address the ball and draw back my cue. Recognizing the shot as one with high scratch potential, I decide to slightly cheat the pocket as I set my aiming line. Just as I take the shot, Colette leans low against the table, her blouse dangling so I see both the profile of her breasts and the fact that she doesn't wear a bra. The distraction sends the cue ball off-course, to carom off the side and into the sewer of the opposite corner pocket. The scratch costs me the game. Accompanied by gasps and laughs from the spectators, I lay the cue on the table and join the ranks of the defeated.

"Who's the queen?" Colette asks.

"Colette's the queen," I reluctantly voice. My triumphant adversary blows me a kiss and rests her cue against the wall. Instead of awaiting the challenge of the next contestant, she pats my shoulder and leads me away from the table.

"Care to join me for a smoke?" she asks.

"I don't smoke," I say, in a once-bitten, twice-shy tone that indicates my displeasure with Colette's Machiavellian tactics.

"Well, maybe you need some fresh air then."

The mention of fresh air makes me perceive just how stifling the bar had grown, and I notice the dampness of perspiration on my shirt.

"Fresh air sounds good," I agree.

We amble out of the bar and across the grassy plateau to the parking area. From the glove box of a beat-up sedan, Colette obtains a pack of cigarettes and a lighter. Meanwhile, as my eyes adjust to the night, I gasp in sudden wonder. A thousand fireflies appear congregated among the grass and upon the metal surfaces of the parked cars. Then, my perception shifts, and I recognize the fireflies as dew drops that gleam diamond with reflected starlight—diamond, but also emerald and sapphire, as beads of yellow and green sparkle among the white. When I turn my gaze upward, the source of the lightshow spreads across the night: the Milky Way like a burst of spray paint, Sirius outshining its neighbors, and a hint of the Southern Cross low on the horizon. The stars of Micronesia dance as though plugged in to a celestial current. In disregard of the dew and an occasional buzzing mosquito, I lean my back against Colette's car and try to remember if I've ever seen a night as stunning as the one that now envelopes my gaze.

"Beautiful, isn't it?" Colette says. Her cigarette brightens and dims as she drags and exhales.

"Beautiful and beyond," I say. "I've never seen anything like it."

For a while, in silence, we watch the stars. Colette sits with her leg against mine, and the soft warmth almost, but not quite, draws me to her. Her coquettish smile suggests a spirited lass eager for a kiss, but her eyes pool with the sadness of a woman tormented by time. Feeling awkward, I move away slightly and fill the gap with conversation.

"So, what's with all the Colette's-the-queen stuff?" I ask. "Does anybody else get similar accolades?"

Colette sighs but indulges my interrogation. "In my younger days I competed in beauty contests," she says. "I actually made runner-up for Miss Texas."

Sucking her cigarette, she assesses the impact of this information. "You don't believe me?" she asks accusingly.

Opening the car door, she rummages through the glove box and produces a postcard-size photo for scrutiny. "That's me on Galveston Beach," she says. Illumined by the car's interior light, a bikini-clad brunette stares back from the picture.

"Miss Texas, huh?" I ponder.

"Runner up," she clarifies. "But the girl who beat me cheated. She was having an affair with one of the judges. Really, I should have won."

"Colette the beauty queen," I muse. "So, how did you end up here?

"How does anybody end up anywhere?" she sighs, after a long pause in which she returns her attention to the stars.

The question dangles, rhetorically ripe, a doorway to philosophical inquiry where simple questions invoke complex answers.

Collette laughs the half-amused, half-bitter laugh of the jaded. "We don't control the circumstances of our lives. One day I woke up and found I was nothing special. So, I cling to that little place where confidence still resides—sometimes that's a pool table at Club Cupid."

Confronted by the cynicism in her words, I retreat into silence, contemplating circumstance. From a distant yard, the sound of a barking dog comes upon the breeze. Staccato barks tun into yelps that suddenly cut short. Remembering Gavin's conversation about Fringe cuisine, I wonder if an island family decided to have dog for dinner, and think that in the panoply of predicament, the life of a dog on an island of dog-eaters holds a particular poignancy.

"Pot roast," I mutter, giving voice to my thought.

"Pot roast?" Colette inquires, puzzled.

"The dog, barking in the distance. . .I heard it yelp and go quiet. So, I wondered if an island family decided to eat dog for dinner. I hear they taste like pot roast."

"Who told you that?" Colette asks.

I tell her about Gavin and his lifestyle experiment.

"That's interesting. I always thought they tasted like goat." She laughs and gives my hand a squeeze. "Actually, I know some good dog recipes. Why don't you come over for dinner sometime?"

Taking a last drag on her cigarette, she heads back to the bar.

Excerpt from a Diary, August 1999:

Nervous anticipation knots my stomach on the first day of school as I enter the classroom and survey the dark faces that hesitantly meet my eyes. I take a professorial stance behind the lectern, clink open my briefcase, and produce the totems of my craft: white-board marker, textbook, syllabi. After distributing the syllabi, which the students peruse with expressions of curiosity and incomprehension, I clear my throat and address the class. "Welcome to Expository Writing 1," I begin. "During the next 18 weeks, this class will develop your writing and critical thinking abilities in preparation for coursework at a 4-year university." At the mention of "critical thinking" and "university," the students' eyes glaze over. A wiry boy seated in the back row gets up, shuffles nonchalantly toward the open window, and expunges a mass of betel-stained saliva onto the grass outside. The flow of my voice loosens the knot in my stomach, so I ignore the behavior and warm to my lecture, expounding upon the value of English Composition and its place within Higher Education. Somewhere amid my enthusiasm, forty minutes elapse and I forget to take roll. Bringing my lecture to a finale, I give the first homework assignment—a textbook reading intended to illustrate the rhetorical concepts underlying the first essay project. "Any questions?" I ask, pleased with the way I managed the course introduction with nary a stammer.

Following a brief silence, a girl hesitantly raises her hand. "What ees homework?" she asks.

The question forces me to re-think a semester's worth of lesson-plans.

Snapshot of an Expos I class. The camera-ready expressions reveal a social enthusiasm typically restrained in Micronesian youth, whose cultural background encouraged an innate shyness that frequently made classroom discussion difficult. Adding to the communication challenge was the code of non-verbal cues (a quick lifting of the eyebrows might signal "yes," for example) which constituted its own special language. From a pedagogical perspective, the cultural differences often meant lesson plans required a re-design so that students could find a meaningful connection to the subject matter.

Chapter 4: A Ruin with a View

Star-shimmered nights, afternoon thunderstorms, the mists of Fern Cove in the morning—nature's changing face provides a clockwork of beauty that helps stabilize my first week of teaching. Faced with multiple challenges, I undergo a crisis of spirit. Many of the students barely understand me, and others have difficulty grasping the purpose of the class or college in general.

"Why we here?" some baseball-capped students from Chuuk ask. "Dis class ees stupid."

"The government wants you educated. College will help you get jobs," I explain.

"What jobs?" they challenge. "Why we want jobs? We can go to our island and fish."

Such sentiments underlie the glassy-eyed apathy that greets my lecture on the fundamentals of essay organization. Add to this a nostalgic e-mail from my ex-fiancée, stating that we could salvage our relationship if I only came back to California, and I feel a deep sense of dislocation. By the weekend, I react in the way I usually do to such circumstances: I hunger for surf.

Queries about a vehicle for my wave hunt lead me to the Palms Hotel. Situated on one of Kolonia's mongrel-dog side streets, the hotel, with peeling paint and debris-strewn outdoor bar, caters to a guest population of zero. Accordingly, I hope to talk the presumably business-starved owner into giving me a favorable rate on a rental car.

Sammy, the hotel owner's son, offers me a deal. Hire him as a guide, he promises, and he'll drive me to some waves. Go alone, he warns, and I'll find only flat tires and grief on the rutted, muddy road that leads to the island's far side. For such service, Sammy wants forty dollars. I counter twenty, settle on twenty-five, and on a torpid weekend afternoon, find myself riding shotgun in the hotel van, listening to bass-thumping rap, and following a road that, with each curve beyond Kolonia, progresses deeper into a King Kong landscape.

With baggy pants that hang off his waist, a garish necklace of fake gold, and hand gestures timed to the beat, Sammy imitates MTV rappers whose videos play on island T.V. sets. Yet Sammy retains island habits, spitting gobs of red betel juice out the window and driving at a pace that enables him to exchange greetings with pedestrian acquaintances.

Wanting "something for the drive," Sammy pulls over at a roadside stand where smiling kids, sheltering under a palm-thatched roof, sell coconuts and breadfruit. With horn-honks and a holler of "Daisyleen!" Sammy conjures from the shadows of the stand a heavy-set woman, her eyes like crimson bulbs behind the burnt tassels of her bangs. As the woman shuffles toward us, Sammy asks me for five dollars. I reluctantly hand him a bill, wondering how much such stops, repeated at other stands, might add to the day's expense. In exchange for the money, the woman hands Sammy two joints bursting at the seams with Pohnpeian pot. Crimson bulbs focused on me, she asks if I want to be her "mehnwei husband." She then speaks to Sammy in rapid-fire Pohnpeian, setting them both to laughter—she with a wild cackle, he with nervous grunts.

Resuming the drive, Sammy explains that Daisyleen may look scary, but grows some great marijuana.

"What did she say to you?" I ask. "You look a bit nervous."

"She told me she would make the rain fall so hard we would have to turn around and spend the day romancing her."

"How can she do that?"

"Witchcraft," Sammy says.

We drive a while in silence as I ponder both the information and the matter-of-fact way Sammy presented it. Then, curious about Pohnpeian vocabulary, I ask, "what's mehnwei?"

"White skin. Like you . . . mehnwei!" he says, lighting one of the joints.

Not much later, somewhere between the time the Micronesian pot asserts its effect and the spot where the pavement gives way to rutted dirt, the first cloudburst begins. Through dark

Roadside vending stand with dedicated management team. On an island whose lush foliage makes fruit free for the plucking, such operations prove more convenient than necessary, but in the calculus of commerce, smiling kids make an irresistible advertising ploy.

curtains of rain, Sammy drives by Braille, navigating past potholes that chomp at the van's underside. A series of scenes move by like a slideshow: skeletal dogs darting from unseen lairs to attack our tires; palm-roofed cabanas, where shirtless men mash roots upon stones; and lofty basalt crags crying waterfall tears.

"It don't often rain this hard," Sammy mutters, eyes glued to the windshield for a better view.

He puts the wipers on overdrive. Suddenly, swerving to avoid a wayward pig, Sammy slides our rear tires into a ditch; the accelerator produces only a spray of mud. For a brief, lightning-lit second, the pig seems to laugh with a human face.

"It's her! Sammy shouts. "It's Daisyleen's face!"

"We probably saw a trick of the lightning," I reason, certain the marijuana also played a role.

"No way," Sammy replies, his gangster-rap image replaced by a white-knuckle grip on the steering wheel. "We gotta turn back. Who knows what else dat witch can do?"

Mustering a stern tone, I mention that I paid him to find some waves. "I don't care about witches, rain, or pigs. I care about waves. Understand?"

Eventually, Sammy calms down, but demands his original fee as the price to continue the journey.

"If we count the marijuana, I've already paid more than we agreed," I protest.

"Forty dollars," he insists. "My original fee."

"Fine."

The negotiations restore the van's traction, and the pig, its visage pig-like once again, watches us resume our journey. Eventually the rain lessens, relaxing to a drizzle. Out the driver's window, I catch glimpses of Pohnpei's broad lagoon; on the passenger side, a continuous thicket of ferns, palms, and flowering shrubs drip water from their leaves. After a time, the foliage draws back, and we come to a ravine with a forest pool tucked among the slopes. Behind the pool, a shimmering cascade, spreading a silver apron over the crags and ledges of the underlying basalt, completes the postcard scene.

"Kepirohi Falls," Sammy says. "You should see it in sunshine, when Peace Corps girls arrive wearing bikinis. Do you like Peace Corps girls?"

"Right now, I'd like some waves," I answer.

Just past the waterfall, Sammy turns down a narrow path, parks in the front yard of a cinder-block house, and, after paying the residents a few dollars (which I again supply), gestures for me to follow. Intrigued by the "mehnwei" carrying a surfboard, several small children tag along.

"Surfing man! Surfing man!" they chant, palms curled in imitation of a breaking wave. "Hawaii five-oh!"

With gawks and giggles, they follow while Sammy leads me down a crushed coral-and-gravel walkway that traverses the mangrove swamp. Among the mangroves, the air grows stifling. The kids turn homeward, leaving us to the muffled sound of our footsteps and the occasional plink of water dripping from branches into puddles. Just off the path, in muddy alcoves of shadow, stone slabs begin to appear. Some, like fallen trees, lie wrapped in vines. Others, assembled in groups, recall the foundations of ancient dwellings. Sammy stops and bows his head before continuing.

"Here we come to da ruins of Nan Madol," Sammy says. "Walk carefully among da stones."

Following Sammy, I pass through a last thicket of mangroves, then halt, awestruck. A group of ruins, their foundations and walls composed of interlocked basalt pillars and slabs, stand before me. The largest ruin, separated from the path by a small canal, resembles a giant fortress of black stone logs. Each log, a massive hexagonal basalt crystal, seemingly derived

Kepirohi Falls. Shattered by its passage over the uneven cliff face, the water forms countless rivulets that, like balls in a pachinko machine, bounce and ping through a mellifluous descent.

from some magician's experiment in lithic technology, fits smoothly with its neighbors in precise arrangement. Some, bus-length and boasting the diameter of tractor tires, clearly weigh many tons, inspiring me to ponder the method behind their transport and placement. As I marvel at the stones, the sound of surf comes to my ears. Drawn to the edge of the ruins, where a stone wall borders the sea, I see a panorama of ocean and offshore islets. Across a small lagoon, playful waves rise, peak, and peel along a slab of reef.

"OK?" Sammy inquires, gesturing toward the surf.

"It'll do," I judge.

In truth, Nan Madol presents one of the most exotic environments I've ever encountered and, regardless of the surf, I consider the journey worthwhile. The prospect of putting my surfboard to its intended use spurs me to apply sunscreen and put on my sun-protective lycra jersey. Another set rises, peels, and raises my enthusiasm a notch. The last wave, its surface a shimmer of sunbeams that suddenly poke through the clouds, throws a lip toward the shallows, forming a hollow cylinder that terminates in an exhalation of mist.

"Actually, it will do just fine," I say, amending my earlier comment.

I step off the stone wall into the sea and begin a paddle across the lagoon. After several strokes, I look back to gauge my progress. Sammy, wreathed in marijuana smoke, sits in contemplation, while the ruins loom silent behind. Viewed from the water, Nan Madol's massive scope grows more apparent. In addition to the ruins behind Sammy and hidden among the mangroves, others rise as stone islands in an adjacent bay. Continuing toward the surf, I see the remains of structures submerged in the blurry depths beneath me. A feeling grows that with every stroke across the lagoon, I violate further a sacred realm of ancient priests. I picture using my surfboard as a shield

Nan Madol, with "log cabin" stone arrangement clearly visible. One cornerstone of Nan Dowas, the largest ruin, is estimated to weigh 50 tons. The ruins, promoted in tourist brochures as the "Venice of the Pacific," spread across 150 acres and comprise Micronesia's most important archeological site, a status which, prior to FSM independence, conferred upon them U.S National Historic Landmark recognition.

against the spears of muscled warriors that materialize from the mangroves to punish trespassers. Dispelling such fears, the sun, with newfound vigor, paints a rainbow over a trio of islets offshore. The water, bathtub warm, laps playfully against my board, inviting me onward. The rain clouds part, opening a view of volcanic ramparts, the bulwark of Pohnpei's southern shore. Other than Sammy, now a speck among the ruins, I observe nothing of humanity. Of sound, my ears register only the slosh of my paddling and the crash of surf.

Once in the surf zone, I see what gives form to the breakers: an orange-red plateau of coral, its edge dropping cliff-like toward deeper water. Urchins and anemones cling to its surface, their spines and tentacles a promise of pain lest I accidentally brush the reef. As an approaching set dredges water off the shallows, I take a few strokes seaward, trying to distance myself from the impact zone. The reef gives me a caution out of proportion to the surf, which, averaging shoulder high, might elicit wild abandon back home in California. I let the wave pass, and seeing another further out, angle to what I judge as the take-off spot.

The wave begins to crest. I muscle toward the trough, stand to the hiss of water rushing under my board, and race the lip of a tapering wall about thirty yards long. A series of quick pumps, arcing my board's edge along the wall, give me speed. After a slicing turn off the bottom, I extend a vertical trajectory up the face, hang for a weightless second as the bottom of my board smacks a shower of crystal spray off the lip, and let the forward surge of the crest push me down. Raising the stakes, the wave breaks faster and sucks water off reef that, now ridiculously shallow, bares a vision of anemones and urchins waiting to extract a toll. Meeting the terms, I trim tight midway down the face, and use the suction off the shallows to slingshot me through the critical section. I kick out as the remainder of the comber fizzles to foam. Though only seconds in duration, the ride provides a dose of adrenaline that I want repeated, and I paddle back for more.

Over the next hour, my rides proceed much as my first: a quick takeoff, followed by a snappy turn and a sled run over the inside reef. The break, a short peak that peels toward a semi-channel, reminds me of Hawaiian summer waves — only without the Hawaiians who greet unwanted travelers with a stink-eye or a fist. Conditioned psychologically for California, where even mediocre surf draws a crowd, I follow the mantra of the proverbial kid in the candy store, grabbing every piece I can. Eventually, acclimatized to the solitude, I adopt a more selective approach, choosing only the tastier morsels while enjoying the beauty of others. Some waves, their lips paper thin, resemble sculptures of delicate glass, crafted temporarily from the sea before breaking. Others trail faint halos of color, as whispers of offshore breeze blow from their crests a salty mist, each drop a prism for light from the afternoon sun. Gliding alongside such a vision, I trim high upon the face, placing my hand in the mist, trying to touch the rainbow.

Gradually, and then rapidly, a lower tide changes the conditions. Currents swirl through the take-off spot. Waves break not as peeling peaks but as walls collapsing all at once. A new surf zone appears further out to sea, over a reef previously too deep to influence the swell. Instead of surfable waves, the new reef produces only random cascades of whitewater that gasp and re-form as smaller, lumpy breakers closer to shore. The re-forms, however, allow only drop-ins toward exposed coral. The light also fades, as the sun passes west behind the island's central peaks, which extend long arms of shadow seaward. Brooding on the shoddy conditions, I consider the good fortune that led me to arrive when I did. Labeling Nan Madol a high-tide-only spot, I resolve to time any future sessions accordingly, and head toward

Nan Madol: another empty fun one spins off during high tide and sumertime (July-October) Southwest winds. Though playful compared to the power of Pohnpei's more exposed reef passes, the break offers an unmatched scenic mystery, which, combined with the occasional down-the-line section, leaves a session here etched upon the memory.

the ruins, my stomach gurgling with hunger.

On my return across the lagoon, I notice bursts of white flash on the horizon beyond the offshore islets. I sit on my board for a better look, and recognize the bursts, which focus consistently to the left of the outermost islet, perhaps a mile or more distant, as surf breaking along a gap in Pohnpei's barrier reef. Aware that such gaps, or reef passes, can produce quality surf, I scrutinize the vista, but distance and fading light thwart my vision. I resume my paddle, making a mental note to investigate the islets on a future exploration. Suddenly, a dull thud sends vibrations along the length of my board. Looking into the water, I expect to find a hidden pinnacle of reef. Instead I brush cheeks with a sea turtle. Before swimming on, the turtle regards me curiously, eyes full of numinous nuance. A few moments later, I encounter another turtle, whose mottled shell scrapes my fingers when I paddle by. Soon, I find myself surrounded by sea turtles, all of them heading in a procession to the ruins like acolytes on a mysterious mission. The sight leaves me spellbound until I reach the seawall, where I find Sammy reclined on a chair-like stone. Eyes and teeth red from an afternoon of marijuana and betel, Sammy greets me with a yawn, but rises quickly to his feet.

Etching a memory of the session and geography in my mind, I look back to the water. Beyond the trio of islets, I again detect a flash of white, dimmer in the twilight, indicative of breaking surf. "What about that far island?" I ask. "Any waves there?"

"Dat place Nahpali," he replies. "Lots of sharks. To get there, you need a boat."

Mulling the distance and sharks, I reach a similar conclusion.

"Without a boat, surfing very difficult," Sammy advises. "Here at Nan Madol, waves come close to shore. Everywhere else, you must cross a wide lagoon to reach them."

According to legend, sea turtles played a role in the annual religious rites conducted by high priests of the Saudeleurs, who kept the turtles in special pools adjacent to the Nan Madol temples.

"Right," I murmur, sliding my feet into my sandals for the walk back.

"Bad to linger here after dark," Sammy advises, turning to leave.

Indeed, twilight gives the ruins a somber character. Gaps between jumbled stones look like mournful eyes, and occasional drips into mangrove puddles sound like footsteps. Once across the canal by the largest ruin, Sammy turns, bows his head, and speaks a quiet word in the island tongue.

"What did you say?" I ask.

"Kalangan," Sammy says. "A thank-you for da guardians."

"Guardians?" I inquire.

"Sprits of da Saudeleurs, rulers who once lived here. Sometimes they come back, appearing as balls of light among da ruins, or as sea creatures, like turtles or sharks, who return at dusk to protect their city."

After a halting try at pronunciation, which Sammy corrects, I too offer a quiet "Kalangan," and follow Sammy in silence on the gloomy path to the van.

During our return to Kolonia, night submerges the road in inky black, which the beams of our headlights prod like feeble antennae. Sammy, submerged in his music, dons his rap persona. An occasional cabana, lit by hanging lanterns, emerges along the roadside, framing gathered islanders in oases of light. "Sakau time!" Sammy says as we pass a particularly crowded cabana.

"How about dinner time," I add, as my hunger grows insistent.

"Sakau can fix your hunger," Sammy says. "A few bowls will numb your stomach. A few more will numb everything else."

Eager to introduce me to the island custom, Sammy takes us on a jungle detour, at whose end, he promises, awaits a sakau

79

bar "like da old days." We bass-thump our way down a grassy path, charge a gauntlet of groping branches, and pull up to a clearing where Sammy stops the van by a group of haphazardly-parked cars. Just beyond the cars, wan red Christmas lights, strung between poles, battle the darkness over a row of picnic tables and benches. A clapboard shack, surrounded by jungle, suggests the residence of the bar's proprietor. Grafted to the benches, patrons make monotone conversation or stare zombie-like into the shadows. "Yo Rickson!" Sammy hollers, heading to a table where a pudgy young man sits quietly.

"Hey Sammy! Where you been all day? Da girlfriend lookin' for you. . ."

"Which one?" Sammy asks as we sit down.

"Yo mama!" Rickson exclaims, throwing a punch at Sammy's arm.

Rickson and I exchange introductions. Sammy asks me to place on the table sakau money for the three of us. Accepting as a given the rising cost of having Sammy as my guide, I deposit the rest of my cash—all ten dollars of it—in Sammy's fingers.

"I can put in somethin'," Rickson offers. "I can drink a lot of sakau."

"Sakau pow-wow!" Sammy says, adding a phrase in Pohnpeian. The two begin an animated banter in the island tongue.

Surveying the scene, I notice money on other tables. A young girl, her hair in pigtails, plies a circuit among the patrons, collecting the offerings in a rusty coffee can. In a space apart from the tables, two shirtless men, their brown backs shiny with perspiration, kneel over a large flat stone, where one man places an arm-length strip of wet hibiscus bark. Smoothing the bark with his hand, the man melds the fibers into a sheet. Soaked pepper roots, spread upon the sheet like glistening worms, then serve as filling for a hibiscus-wrap. Twisted into a rope and wrung like a wet towel, the hibiscus-wrap soon drips a trickle of muddy goop. The entire process, repeated a few times, squeezes out enough liquid to fill a large bowl made of coconut shell. As one squeezer fills a bowl, the second begins the process anew, keeping the production line steady. Meanwhile, the little girl carries the filled coconut bowl to the tables, where the patrons pass it around. Those who wish to drink clasp the bowl with both hands and raise it slowly to their lips. Eyes closed, the drinker grimaces, takes a long swig, and drools a trail of dirty slime from lips to chin.

When the sakau bowl comes to me, I take an ambitious sample of the contents, and discover that grimaces and drool result as much from physical reaction as custom. An alkaline bitterness makes the drink curdle the taste buds. Swallowed, the liquid leaves numbness in its wake, while a mucous-textured residue clings to the tongue and triggers salivation. After subsequent swigs, my numb lips can't find the rim of the bowl. I too dribble slime and saliva. Closing my eyes helps me forget that sakau has the visual appeal of mud. However, I can't forget my growing concern that the concoction must subject the drinker to numerous septic hazards. The coconut bowl, I surmise, must contain equal parts sakau and saliva from prior mouths. My concern fades, however, as I succumb to a benumbed nonchalance.

"This feels good," Sammy sighs.

"This feels like your mama," Rickson says. He again throws a punch at Sammy's arm, but the punch goes astray, and Rickson nearly topples off his seat. He and Sammy roil with laughter. An old man sitting nearby quiets them.

"Ssh!" the old man admonishes. "Lemme listen. Da stone gonna sing now."

In the preparation area, a second shirtless pair of men arrives with a bundle of fresh pepper roots. The sakau squeezers put aside their hibiscus bark and pick up some grapefruit-sized rocks. The second pair joins them with rocks of their own, completing a rudimentary percussion quartet who tune up by tapping their rocks against the sakau stone. The fresh pepper roots, spread evenly atop the stone, now receive a rhythmic pounding. The stone rings like a bell. One burly pounder maintains a steady beat while the others add syncopations. The singing stone, red Christmas lights, and my fellow drinkers' zombie expressions make for a surreal atmosphere, into which a growing pressure in my bladder rudely intrudes. I have to pee.

Sammy, pointing toward the trees, answers my request for directions to the bathroom. On the edge of light, a ply-wood shed with a shower curtain for a door stands out from the grasping jungle. Acknowledging Sammy's directions, I rise, only to find my legs sakau-numb and wobbly. I grab for the table's edge, miss, and stumble to the ground. Sammy and Rickson, laughing at my troubles, again receive a scolding by the old man, who shushes them as I proceed haltingly to the shed.

Pushing aside the shower curtain, I discover the "bathroom" already hosts an occupant—a red centipede about ten inches long. My intrusion spurs the centipede toward my sandaled feet. Fearful of its potentially painful bite, I step back in haste, and nearly stumble again. The prospect of trying to pee while fending off a hostile centipede makes me reconsider my bathroom adventure. Saving such a battle for a time less influenced by sakau, I return to the tables.

"Too numb to pee?" Sammy asks, as the pounders finish their percussion and the patrons resume subdued conversations.

"A centipede tried to attack me," I explain.

"A centipede in the bathroom?" Rickson asks in a serious tone. "You sure?"

I nod.

"What did it look like?"

"Like a centipede," I say.

"Did it have just a little short stub of an antennae?" Rickson prods

"Maybe," I say. Before I can clarify that my haste to exit the bathroom prevented a close examination of the bug's distinguishing characteristics, Rickson grows agitated.

"Oh man. This means trouble!" Rickson exclaims.

"What you worry about?" Sammy questions. "We got centipedes all over da island."

"That centipede came lookin' just for me," Rickson claims.

"You serious?" Sammy inquires.

"Lucky for me, Jacques saw it first," Rickson says. "Now I know not to go in there."

"What you talkin' about?"

"Well," Rickson begins, "you know that crazy lady who sells marijuana at the fruit stand?"

Sammy, eyes wide, nods for Rickson to continue.

"About a month ago, I stopped at the fruit stand for a joint. The lady told me that if I didn't marry her, her pet centipede would hunt me down in the bathroom at my most vulnerable moment and bite me in my most vulnerable place."

Sammy, grimacing, looks at his crotch as he contemplates the effect of centipede venom on a certain part of the male anatomy.

"At first, I didn't think about it," Rickson continues. "Who ever heard of a pet centipede?"

Sammy considers the question. "I nevah hear of a pet centipede," he concludes.

"Right," Rickson says. "So, I not worry. But, about a week later, as I sat on the toilet in my Auntie's house, a long red centipede squirmed under the bathroom door. It ran circles 'round my feet and rushed back out. Second time happened just last night, in the bathroom at Club Cupid. Centipede just sat on

83

top of the paper towel dispenser and wiggled its antennae."

"Hmmm," Sammy grunts, still a bit skeptical. "How do you know it was da same centipede? Coulda just been random coincidence, no?"

Rickson shakes his head. "I tellin' you. It was the SAME CENTIPEDE!"

"Dat sounds scary," Sammy agrees, shaken by the tale. "What you gonna do?"

"I have a plan," Riskson whispers. "I gotta stay away from bathrooms. When I need to go, I'll head for da bushes instead."

Sammy narrows his eyes and rubs his chin, evidently pondering the complexity of Rickson's problem and its proposed solution. "Good idea!" he says finally, excitedly nodding his approval.

"Think so?" Rickson asks, in need of reassurance.

"Sure," Sammy affirms. "Dat witch say her pet centipede would look for you in da bathroom, yeah?"

"That's what she told me."

"Well, you stay away from bathrooms, da centipede won't find you!"

With high-fives and grins, the two friends cheer their strategy and its potential to neutralize Daisyleen's witchcraft. Then, the cheers fade, as Rickson ponders the implications of his plan. "How long I gotta stay away from bathrooms?" he asks, doubt spreading upon his face.

"Maybe forevah," Sammy says, frowning.

The prospect that Daisyleen's witchcraft could prove more difficult to thwart than originally thought drops a pall upon their cheer. Rickson broods further upon his misfortune, and when a fresh bowl of sakau arrives, he drinks heavily, as though the numbing brown liquid, consumed in sufficient quantity, might reveal a solution to his predicament. Sammy casts a glance at me but says nothing of our own encounter with Daisyleen.

Sammy, receiving the bowl next, declines to drink. With a hand against the picnic table to steady himself, he stands abruptly. "Let's go, Jacques," he says. "Just remembered, I gotta get back to da hotel."

"Maybe you think you too good for me now, eh?" Rickson chides. "Maybe, when you need help, I tell people how Sammy treat his friends!"

We leave Rickson to his grumbling and stumble back to the van. Sammy, evidently shaken by Rickson's tale, fumbles to put the keys in the ignition. Meanwhile, my most pressing concern remains the pressure in my bladder. Leaning against the passenger door, I stop to pee, indifferent to any jungle threats— centipede or otherwise—my urine might arouse.

"What you doin'?" Sammy says, agitated by the delay. "We gotta get outta here!" He eyes the bushes warily, as though Daisyleen herself might lurk behind them.

Bladder relieved, I pull myself into the passenger seat, dragging numbness from waist to toe. Sammy looks at me with concern, or at least what passes for concern in the face of a hip-hop wannabe with a penchant for fake bling.

"I think we got big trouble," he informs me. "*You* got big trouble."

"Trouble? Why?"

"Cause dat witch like your white skin. She wants you for a husband! Didn't you hear Rickson's story? Think of what she did to him!"

The van roars to life, and Sammy rends the night in a hasty dash for the hotel, as though I represent some toxic burden he wants to unload as quickly as possible. Where he once drove in confidence, throwing hand gestures to a rap beat, he now drives somberly, a white-knuckle grip on the steering wheel. Grinning, I think of a way to lift the gloom.

"I have a plan," I announce.

"Huh?"

"I know how to deal with Daisyleen."

"You do?" he asks.

"Daisyleen wants me because of my white skin, right?"

"Dat what she say."

"So, suppose I no longer have white skin. . .then she'll no longer want me, right?"

"Probably not," Sammy ponders.

"Well, in that case, *I'll get a tan*."

"Say what?" Sammy says doubtfully.

"I can tan pretty dark," I say. "After a few days of sun, I might not look so mehnwei."

Sammy scratches his chin, and I sense his mind spin the gears of contemplation, evaluating the merits of my plan. "Good idea!" he finally exclaims, grinning broadly.

"Think it'll work?"

"I think so!"

We exchange high-fives. Rap persona restored, Sammy ignites the stereo, and the van flings bass notes into a night still inky black but somehow less menacing.

*   *   *

Excerpt from a Diary, September 1999:

Gradually, the names on my roster match faces, and the faces front personalities.

Marychrist, the Yapese girl who sits in the back corner, seems pulled from the ranks of a South Pacific nunnery. Averting her eyes and hiding her figure in puffy blouses and ankle-length skirts, she wears her modesty as a shield against my efforts to encourage class participation. I wonder what sounds more loudly in her ears — my lecture on thesis statements, or the voice of tradition, telling her to return to the island of stone money, to a life of breadfruit scraping and grass-skirt weaving.

Darwen, the aspiring class clown, refuses to get a textbook, preferring to borrow one from whatever girl-du-jour responds favorably to his antics. His wiry frame draped perpetually in a Junior Seau football jersey, he exudes an air of street savvy. I picture him mingling with equal comfort among the gangs of L.A. or the patrons of a sakau bar, and sense that he regards college as an adventure, made playful by the knowledge that failing out simply means a return to Chuuk, whose broad lagoon teems with fish and invitations to lazy daydreams.

Ehminer, from Kosrae, sits in the front row and takes copious notes. He follows a dress code — shoes, slacks, white collared shirt — that seems applicable only to him. After class one day he approaches me sheepishly and asks if he could borrow two dollars for the taxi. I hand him the bills, but after class I notice that instead of getting a cab, he takes LucyRose — she of the too-tight jeans and coquettish glance, who in another time could have played the role of a beach maiden, her visage a bewitchment to the crews of tall-masted ships — on an outing to the ice-cream stand. He doesn't pay me back, but I keep a few dollars on reserve for him anyway, musing that in Ehminer's studies rest the aspirations of a village.

87

Chapter 5: Adventures in Bird Watching

Teana, the bristle-browed secretary of the Language/Literature Division, sits across from me in the college cafeteria and watches me pick at my lunch of breadfruit, Spam, and steamed rice. Finally, exasperated by the way I gather the pink cubes of Spam into a corner of rejection upon my place, she lashes me with a glare of rebuke.

"Why you not eat? Dat good food!"

"I don't like Spam," I tell her. Despondent after a month of cafeteria cuisine, I think the entire menu deserves a boycott, but I keep the full extent of my food-funk quiet.

"Dat why you so skinny?" Teana scolds. "Why you no like Spam?"

Lunchtime chatter quiets around us. Students peer intently from a nearby table, curious about the guy who "no like Spam."

"I generally try to avoid heavily-processed foods, especially meats," I explain.

"Heavily processed foods?"

"Sure. Back in Los Angeles, lots of health-conscious people avoid processed foods like hot dogs and Spam."

"Who avoid Spam?" Teana asks, incredulous.

"Lots of people, especially in the movie industry. Celebrities, actors. . ."

The words "movie" and "actor" bring a tinge of excitement to Teana's voice and lessen the hostility of her glance. "Movies!" she exclaims. "I love actors. You see dat movie *Titanic*? I love dat actor."

"You mean Leonardo Dicaprio?"

"Yeah! Leonardo Dicaprio. . .he avoid Spam?" Teana inquires.

"Maybe," I say. "I'm not sure."

"Why you not sure?"

"Well, I don't know him personally."

"How come you not know him?" Teana persists. "Don't he come from same place as you?"

"Actually, he does come from Los Angeles," I say, unpacking the trivia from a dusty corner of my mind. "I think he has a place in Hollywood."

"So how come you not know him? You both from same

village!" The rebuke returns, this time motivated by more than displeasure over my avoidance of Spam. The idea that I could dwell in the same geographic region as Leonardo Dicaprio and not know him personally strikes Teana as indicative of some deep flaw in my character.

"How can you live in same village as someone and not know him?" Teana scolds. "I know everyone from my village! I know everyone in dis part of da island!"

I ponder the range of possible responses, searching for a diplomatic way of informing Teana that the "village" of Los Angeles, in its greater metropolitan area, contains over ten million inhabitants, most of whom know only a tiny fraction of the total population. Finally, I limit my defense to a simple answer. "Los Angeles is a pretty big village," I say, shrugging apologetically.

Teana walks off in a huff. Lunchtime chatter resumes. I slog through the remainder of my rice and breadfruit, and the trudge my Spam to the trash.

Later, my colleagues remind me that behind Teana's bristling brows lies the concern of a mother hen — a hen, albeit, given to dark mood swings. The fact that Teana views the Language Arts faculty as her personal flock presents both a benefit and a drawback. Through her extensive web of acquaintances, faculty in her good graces can find themselves privy to the inner sanctum of island society. Conversely, those lacking such graces might find themselves victimized by subtle manifestations of island ill will.

The next day, hopeful for Teana's good graces, I bring an offering: a four pack of Starbuck's Frappuccinos, purchased at a discount from the clearance rack of a Kolonia market. Thinking the beverage might give Teana a reprieve from the stale coffee normally prevalent in the Language Arts office, I place it obsequiously on her desk. In return I get scowls and silence.

Eventually, my colleagues advise me that the path to

Teana's good graces lies not through token trinkets but through a more serious endeavor: a business deal.

"Let Teana help buy you a car," Mayra suggests.

The idea offers a chance to improve not only my social standing, but my lifestyle. My Los Angeles upbringing, which links happiness with the ability to flash chrome and a lusty stereo before one's fellow commuters, makes me feel deprived without a vehicle of my own. My current reliance on taxis, neighbors' cars, and third-party profiteers, at first a novel aspect of my island life, now irks me daily. Teana's web of connections, my colleagues contend, will yield an island jalopy at the best price.

Perhaps seeing in my car-search the prospect of a middleman's fee, Teana lights up, and gives me a smile slick with scheming—but a smile nonetheless. I take it as an invitation to potential good graces.

"So, you need car!" she says, rubbing her palms together. "How much you wanna spend?"

The deal she brokers leads me to one of Kolonia's back alleys, where, beckoning me into a trash-strewn yard, a shop owner unveils an old Mazda, its decrepit frame like the carcass of dead beetle shriveled by the sun. Upon inspection, the Japanese sedan spews the white smoke indicative of burning engine oil, while its undercarriage bears numerous dents, testament to bruising encounters with island potholes. Nevertheless, the sedan conveys the air of a grizzled veteran who takes bruises in stride. I envision it as a passport to adventure, and back my hope in the car's prospects with two-thousand dollars of my savings from summer teaching. Predictably, as I drive up the road from Kolonia to campus, the car tests my faith with a new malady: a bad rear-wheel bearing, which contributes the sound of grating metal to the car's idiosyncrasies. I accept it as a minor annoyance and wear a smile as I pull up to campus in a chaos of white smoke and rear-axle rheumatism.

92

"So, how you like car?" Teana asks, as I stroll past the Language Arts Office.

"Just fine," I say.

"You sure?" Teana queries. "If car give you trouble, I know good mechanic!" Her eyes gleam with the prospect of middleman's fees yet to come.

Over the next few days, the sound of grating metal gets louder. I speculate that maybe Teana and the shop owner conspired to sell me a lemon, but I put a bold face on the matter. Like Sisyphus enduring his burden, I vow that whatever hardship the car may inflict upon me, I won't give those who relish my suffering the satisfaction of hearing me complain.

"You sure you like car?" Teana persists.

"Absolutely," I stoically affirm. "In fact, I plan to take it exploring this weekend."

"Where you go?" she demands, surprised by my plan.

Though prudence dictates staying close to the safety net of Kolonia's mechanics and repair shops, I recall my journey to Nan Madol a few weeks prior, and picture myself as an intrepid explorer, in the mold of Indiana Jones, roaming the ruins of Pohnpei's Southeast corner. The romanticism which led me to purchase the car reasserts itself. "Maybe I'll go explore around Nan Madol," I say.

"Nan Madol?" Teana whispers, sucking in her breath. "You no go! You stay away from Nan Madol!" she admonishes, voice quaking. Her suddenly wide eyes express a genuine concern. "Dat place dangerous."

I tell her how, weeks prior, I visited Nan Madol with a guide, and encountered nothing worse than rainbows and sea turtles.

"You lucky," Teana says. "Dat place dangerous. . . especially at night." The news that I not only visited Nan Madol once, but intend to again, mobilizes her mood. "You college teacher!" she scolds. "You suppose to plan lesson, not explore!"

When I ask for details about the danger, she reluctantly reveals that the mysterious ruins represent a domain of ghosts. A night among the stones exposes the unwary visitor to wandering balls of light, the spiritual manifestation of ancient sorcerers powerful enough to float massive basalt crystals through the air like feathers.

Girded by the fantasy of surf exploration, I dismiss her concerns, and with hubristic confidence, promise to depart the ruins before nightfall.

Accordingly, one September weekend, I grind my way down the road to the island's Southeast corner, pay the local family a nominal use fee, and hike the mangrove path through the ruins. For the most part, the waves resemble those of my first visit—unspectacular but set in a background of exotic mystery. Like an overlooked schoolgirl, the surf at Nan Madol typically retains a demure demeanor. Casting a binocular-enhanced gaze across the lagoon, I identify the reef pass at Naphali as the area's true seductive beauty, flashing perfect waves that peel along the reef adjacent to the farthest offshore islet. Guarded by distance and a rumor of sharks, Naphali demands from her suitor a greater resourcefulness. Thus, as I stand at Nan Madol's stone seawall and peer seaward, I turn my thoughts to boats.

What happens next nudges me one notch closer to believing in the area's mysterious energy. Whether through serendipity or coincidence, just as I resolve to obtain a boat, a boat appears. Puttering with a light drone, the skiff plies close to the mangrove shore. The boatman, gray-bearded under a broad-brimmed hat, guides his craft toward me, as though by appointment pre-arranged. Motoring close to the seawall, the old man cups his hands to his mouth. "Seen any birds?" he hollers.

"Birds?" I query.

"Especially a Micronesian Kingfisher. I'd really like to see a Micronesian Kingfisher," he says, idling the outboard and drifting close.

"I'd like to get out to that island," I say, gesturing in the direction of Naphali, to whose shore I hope to inveigle a ride.

"You'll find more birds along this shore," the old man advises. His hat, of a canvas safari style, looks standard-issue outdoorsman, but the rest of his attire — full cammo gear, including military boots in a reptilian olive-and-tan pattern — strike me as a bit odd. I half expect to see him toting an M-16 upon his shoulder. Instead, he totes an open binocular case, stuffed with wadded-up papers. Matted hair, falling to grey curls about his shoulders, frames a narrow face with subdued cheekbones, slightly freckled.

Pointing to my surfboard, propped on the stones beside me, I communicate my interest in waves, though I can't tell if my message meets with understanding. "Will you boat me out there?" I ask. "Maybe you'll find some birds, too."

Fingering his beard, the birdwatcher considers the proposition. "I suppose we can look. Mind if I use those binoculars now and then? I seem to have misplaced the pair I was using."

"Use them all you want," I offer, sensing their value as a bargaining chip to the waves.

I float my surfboard and gear toward the boat, which bobs within a few yards of the seawall. Hauling myself over the railing, I swing my legs into the boat, and inadvertently knock my foot against something that produces the sound of clinking glass.

"Don't spill my whiskey!" the old man protests. He gropes for the bottle, takes a swig, and, apparently reassured with the condition of the liquor, props the bottle against the hull. The motor burps, and we putter our way toward Naphali, a trail of bubbles rising slowly in our wake.

"You got a name, son?"

"Jacques," I reply.

"Well, Jack, successful bird watching requires one to keep low and quiet. You won't have much success standing on the rocks like a scarecrow."

"No, I guess not," I finally stammer, wondering whether I should first correct his pronunciation of my name, or his misconception of my interest in bird watching.

"We'll keep our pace slow and steady, so birds don't get scared by our approach," the old man informs me.

While the outboard nudges us languidly across the lagoon, kaleidoscopic scenes distract me from my impatience to reach the surf. Coral plateaus and canyons, forming a submerged scenery of red and purple, slide under the skiff. Above them, schools of darting fish leap from the surface as we motor near. At one point, a great bat shape, darkening the depths like a shadow across a liquid landscape, passes beneath our wake.

"Manta Ray!" I gasp, watching the creature glide among refracted shafts of sunlight.

Reserving his interest for winged creatures of the air, the old man keeps his gaze straight ahead and, puts a finger to his lips. "Quiet," He admonishes. "Don't scare the birds."

The Manta Ray fades from view, and we come to an area of dark blue water that frames our reflection in a background of puffy white clouds. Muttering, the old man addresses me.

"Say, Jack, did you bring a bird chart? I must have misplaced mine."

"Jacques," I correct.

"Er, Jacques," he amends, nursing a gulp from the whiskey bottle. "My mind's a bit foggy right now."

"I didn't bring a bird chart," I say. "Really, I'm not much of a bird watcher."

"Not much of a 'birder,' you mean," he says. "Serious bird watchers prefer the term 'birder.'"

"Well, I'm not really one of those either," I say.

"Now that's a damn shame!" he exclaims, forgetful his own admonition to keep quiet. "Do you realize that this island is a bird watching paradise? Why, just back yonder, before you came aboard, I got a fantastic look at a Pacific Reef Egret, of the black-morph variety. An awesome sight it was, in full breeding plumage!"

"No kidding?" I say, trying to sound politely enthused.

"Oh, that was just the icing on the cake," he says. He leans close, as though making me an accomplice to sensitive information. Whiskey breath, of a concentration a lit match would ignite, burns my nostrils. "Yesterday I saw a Micronesian Starling," he recalls, voice deep with reverence. "Flew up to me and took some papaya straight from my hand."

The bird watcher scrutinizes my face, evaluating my reaction to the news. Perhaps not seeing the proper level of wonder, he grows agitated, his bloodshot eyes shiny with an opaque glaze. His breath comes in wheezing fits. "Can you appreciate what that's like, J . . . J . . ."

"Jacques."

"Well Jacques, I'll tell you what it's like. It's like having a communion with God!" He stares me down, no doubt considering my under-appreciation of the avian world as heathen ignorance.

Apart from the bird watcher's inebriation—a condition with unpredictable consequences in the tropical heat—the passion for bird watching, conveyed with the aggression of a proselytizer, makes me nervous. The old man seems as likely to hit me over the head with his whiskey bottle as to deliver me to the surf. Then, I second-guess my feelings. After all, at times in my past, in the company of friends who later mocked me, hadn't I spoken of surfing with the same reverence that the bird watcher applies to his pastime? I squelch my misgivings and manage a contrite reply.

"I never thought about it like that," I confess.

"Damn shame," he mutters.

Gradually, our destination looms larger. Naphali Island raises a deserted margin of beach around a stand of palms. Unlike Pohnpei itself, where mangrove swamp surrounds rainforest slopes, the lagoon islets offer a limited geography of sand under a palm canopy. Fallen coconuts and palm fronds dot the beach, while shadows gather behind the palm trunks. Breaking surf paints white foam into the blue gap of the reef pass. Soon, the surf's breath grows audible, providing a sibilant counterpoint to the outboard's mechanical drone. My anticipation builds. Meanwhile, ignorant of my surf quest, the old man uses the binoculars to survey Naphali's tree line. As he does, a bird emerges from the palms and wings its silhouette against the sky.

"Frigate bird, by the looks of it," he announces, adjusting the focus on the binoculars. "Fine specimen, too."

Eager for me to admire the frigate bird, he hands me the binoculars.

"Mark its speed!" the bird watcher exclaims. "Mark the graceful manner of its flight!"

"Beautiful," I say, focusing on the surf, the true object of my interest. The waves off Naphali cavort along the reef and leap toward the shallows with acrobatic exuberance. My anticipation turns to adrenaline.

"I can guess where it's headed," the bird watcher says, pointing back toward the mangroves—a direction that would take me farther from, rather than closer to, the surf.

I know where I'm headed, I think, confident I could paddle the remaining distance to Naphali.

Seized by ornithologic obsession, the bird watcher steers the skiff in pursuit of the frigate bird.

"Just a moment!" I exclaim, disturbed by our detour. "Let me get out of the boat!"

"Get out of the boat? Whatever for? You'll not find a more handsome frigate bird than that fellow yonder!"

I drop the binoculars and grab my surfboard. "Just come pick me up on your way back," I holler, leaping overboard.

"Damn shame," the bird watcher mouths. Intent upon his quarry, he opens the throttle. The outboard, flinging foam, transforms into an aft-thruster vocalizing the excitement of the chase.

Frigate Bird. Known to range great distances over the world's tropical oceans, frigate birds have large wings for their body size, enabling them to soar for long periods, even weeks at a time, on warm updrafts or the steady flow of trade-winds.

In the silence that follows his departure, I settle my gaze on a vast panorama. Filling the horizon, the Pacific spreads its omnipotence. Gathering thunderclouds shoulder a canopy of sky. Uninterrupted by ship, plane, or even a channel buoy to advertise the presence of humanity, the vista conveys a brooding power, and a feeling of isolation envelopes me. The deep water under my board inspires a sense of apprehension, and I paddle softly, lest I provoke some hidden menace. Then, when nothing nips at my hands or feet, I suppress the thought of danger hidden, and focus instead on pleasure visible. Perhaps a five-minute paddle away, swells push into the reef pass, where, adhering to some aquatic blueprint, they break with machine precision. My heart shifts into overdrive, and I forget that by abandoning the skiff, I also abandoned my binoculars, sunscreen, and drinking water.

Approaching an unfamiliar reef, alone and for the first time, even the most intrepid surf explorer might undertake some reconnaissance — investigating the surf zone for possible hazards (an unfriendly protuberance of coral, perhaps), or assessing the direction of the tide. I ignore such precautions, lest I find something that might dampen my enthusiasm for the waves I had staked so much effort to reach.

As a reward for my determination, the surf gods ensure I arrive at the takeoff spot just in time to get a vision of the ideal: a wave that lunges over the shallows, drops a silver curtain from crest to trough, and forms a hollow cylinder spinning toward me. Instinctively, I turn to paddle for it. The cylinder rolls spray, foam, and reflected sunlight into its bosom, and allows only a second for me to drop in and gain my footing. I descend with the lip and, for a weightless second, my board serves as an intermediary between my feet and the air. Scoffing at my persistence, the wave rolls along with freight-train speed, extending a vertical wall down the reef line ahead of me. Off balance from the takeoff, I lack speed to make the section, but set a bold trajectory nonetheless. Briefly, covered by the pitching curl, I get a vision of a spinning liquid tunnel, whose opening, like a distant porthole, looks out upon clouds, sky, and sun-glinted water. In the next instant, the tunnel collapses. A rag doll in a rinse cycle, I endure a series of pelagic punishments, ranging from

a nose full of seawater to a coral-scrape on my leg. Finally, satisfied with my humiliation, the turbulence releases me. I surface, gasping for air. My board, emerging from the froth, floats dutifully nearby. *Hey, at least I landed the drop*, I mutter. Naphali's distant palms look on in silence.

A sudden splash startles me. Barely an arm-length away, a dorsal fin, gray with a white tip, cruises through the foamy aftermath of the wave, followed by a broad black tail that flings water my direction. The dorsal fin—likely that of a gray reef shark, I surmise with an odd detachment—slowly submerges.

In the calculus of danger, instinct usually trumps logic, and few shapes from the animal kingdom catalyze instinctive fears more speedily than the villainous visage of a shark. When encountered up close and unexpectedly, with no aquarium glass or boat hull to intervene, a shark projects a predatory will which highlights all the frailties of the human body. My thoughts turn immediately to self-preservation. Aware that even an investigative nip from the shark could prove serious, I claw for Naphali's shoreline, fearing to look back lest I see the ominous sight of a dorsal fin in close pursuit. Finally, when a small wavelet, serving as an aquatic deus-ex-machina, lifts me forward and deposits me in knee-deep water on the border of the reef pass, the adrenaline thump of my heart subsides.

Finger-size fish scatter away from my feet as I step gingerly among the coral. The water soon reaches only to my ankles, and I discover the shallows of the reef pass conjoin a rock-and-reef tide pool zone that extends from Naphali's beach. Pondering my eviction from the surf, I look seaward once again. With my self-preservation now more assured, I replay the incident through the lens of logic, and see my initial panic as a bit overdone. *Grey reef sharks don't usually prey on humans*, I muse. *If one really wanted to attack, it could have done so without advertising its presence.* Bolstered by these thoughts, I reconsider my retreat.

Naphali Island reef pass on a slightly overhead day. Under the right conditions, most frequent from July to October, Naphali serves up a quality wave. Hazards include isolation, a pitching lip that eagerly throws surfers onto a shallow reef, and murky waters with a reputation for sharks.

Then, I notice a trickle of blood on my shin, no doubt a result of my brush with the coral. With my bloody shin as a variable in the calculus of danger, I come up with unfavorable odds. A perfect set rolls along the reef, but the waves now mock me, like playground children taunting an adversary to whom fences or guards make them immune. Continuing my retreat, I turn my thoughts to the bird watcher and a boat ride back to Nan Madol.

A solitary trail of footsteps marks my journey as I plod Nahpali's shore, scanning the lagoon for a sign of the birdwatcher and his skiff. The beach, lined with shells, offers a treasure trove of trinkets. Occasionally, lured by a colorful specimen, I reach down for a keepsake, and clutch it until the next one catches my eye. Finally, I settle on a conch with glossy tones of pink and white reminiscent of hand-painted china. I check to make sure the shell lacks inhabitants and claim it as a consolation for my sufferings. However, the shiny shell only illuminates an uncomfortable truth: my attempt at surf exploration, begun with such romantic optimism, now amounts to nothing more than a beachcombing expedition. Reluctantly, I recall Teana's admonishment: *"You college teacher! You suppose to plan lesson, not explore!"* The words force me to confront the element of foolishness in my venture, and I vow to approach the rest of the day with more caution.

Plodding further, I come across trinkets of human origin. A plastic ice chest, home to empty beer bottles, lies upon its side. Bleached by the sun, the fibers of a fish net sprout from the sand like mutant grass. Though such items hint at an occasional human visitor to the islet, the lack of footprints other than my own suggests that visitors arrive infrequently at most. Eventually, the oppressive heat and humidity halt my wanderings. Seeking relief, I head toward the palms, prop my board beside me, and recline in the shade afforded by the lattice of fronds overhead. A light breeze whispers past my ears but brings no mention of what I seek—namely, the putter of the bird-watcher's outboard motor. A few minutes' relaxation leads to a catnap, in whose seductive peace the beginnings of a deeper somnolence take root. When I awake—thirsty, sunburned, and startled by the crash of a coconut falling among the detritus nearby—I find the afternoon nearly gone, the sun almost swallowed by Pohnpei's central peaks. In its place, massive clouds, emissaries of atmospheric malevolence, cover the palm grove and lagoon with impending doom. My adventure, I speculate, might entail further suffering.

The squall arrives to a clap of thunder and gusts of wind. Raindrops, advance scouts of a gathering deluge, rattle among the palm grove. The deteriorating weather, added to my increasingly futile wait for the bird watcher, calls attention to an unpleasant prospect: crossing the lagoon by paddling. Worry though I might about fish with sharp teeth, I find less appeal in waiting, hungry and without shelter, for the next happenstance visitor to pluck me from Naphali's deserted shore. Mindful of dorsal fins, I wade into the lagoon until the water reaches my knees, lay prone on my board, and take the first stroke of many that, I hope, will transport me to the far shore before nightfall blinds my path.

As I settle in to my pace, a thin silver wake spins off my rails and gives me a sense of progress. My destination, however, turns increasingly unclear, as grey clouds and curtains of rain obscure the far shore. Fortunately, a skirmish line of palms, standing in stoic formation against the squall, suggests an islet to my left and helps reassure me of my heading. Though my watch shows the passage of time, I soon measure progress not by minutes but arm strokes. Eventually, numbed by the hypnotic monotony of the journey, my mind drifts among random thoughts. I imagine my arms as wings, flapping through the atmosphere of a water world. Fatigue begins to burn in the muscles of my arms and shoulders. The lagoon acquires the semblance of a treadmill, running the same liquid track under me in endless repetition.

At this point, perhaps halfway through my journey, the silhouette of palms fades from view, and I find myself entirely without landmarks. With predatory sense, the squall now intensifies, strafing me with large-caliber raindrops. The wind, raising wavelets that spray salty mist into my eyes, swirls past in eerie howls that resonate with chastisement: *"You college teacher! You suppose to plan lesson, not explore!"* Paddling feels like crawling on the floor of a house built of rain, wind, and cloud. I speculate that my exertions will only lead me in circles, but a countering instinct tells me to keep the wind in my face and plod onward. Onward I plod, until my eyes sting constantly from salt spray and the fatigue in my shoulders extends down my back.

Eventually, my persistence finds reward. The dark walls of the rain house crumble apart. A diffusion of twilight purples spreads over mountain peaks. The squall fades away, and I discern a growth of mangroves extending several hundred yards toward a line of rocks—the stone seawall. I make a final slog in the direction of the ruins, some of which, man-made islets only a few yards square, assert their forlorn architecture in the water nearby. Paddling slowly to avoid obstacles in the murk, I reach the spot where I first saw the bird watcher. With hands pruned from long immersion in the sea, I drag myself onto the stones. Dripping and exhausted, I assess my remaining challenge: finding my way in darkness though the ruins of Nan Madol.

Overhead, twilight purples give way to silver stars, amused spectators to my halting steps. I extend one arm outward as a probe for obstacles, while my surfboard, tucked under the other arm, seems like an anomalous relic from the world of sun and fun, entirely inappropriate to the solemnity of the ruins. Recalling Teana's admonition to avoid Nan Madol after dark, I feel strangely vulnerable. Will the sorcerer spirits materialize, to

107

Located in the rain belt of the Eastern Carolines, Pohnpei is ground zero for sudden squalls, their dark cumulonimbus a moody counterpoint to the bright tropical sun.

demand atonement for my insolence? I stumble forward until a mass of basalt pillars and logs materializes from the darkness. Nan Dowas, the largest of the ruins, with walls seemingly quarried from the night itself, stands before me. Stepping laterally along the façade, I find the gap that marks the path through the interior. I traverse the structure and come to the far wall, where my ears catch the sound of rainwater dripping from stones into the adjacent canal. Just as I extend a foot toward the water, I freeze in my tracks. Here, in the heart of the sorcerers' city, I see them: lights, darting to and fro along the canal's edge. Startled yet curious, I attempt to step back behind the wall, hoping to observe the scene from a more sheltered position. Instead, I slip and sprawl into the canal. The splash summons not a ghost but the voices of startled humans, who illuminate me with flashlights.

"Well of all things. . ." says a gruff voice.

"Where he come from?" queries the shrill tone of a child.

The lights approach. Gradually, I discern their carriers: two figures, one with a net of thick rope, the other bearing long handled tongs. They step close and regard me with wide-eyed surprise, bewildered as much by my presence among the ruins as their presence bewilders me.

"I've heard about ghosts at Nan Madol, but I didn't know they carried surfboards," the gruff voice, belonging to a wiry man, jokes.

"I didn't know they carried flashlights," I reply, sloshing to my feet.

"We're hunting coconut crabs," he explains.

"We already catch two!" says the shrill-voiced boy, pointing a flashlight beam upon the net.

Illumined in the beam, intertwined appendages stretch and contract. I step closer to investigate, and discern a carapace, brownish-purple in the uncertain light, about the size of a dinner plate. Calcareous growths dot its surface.

"Careful!" the man says, as I reach a curious finger toward the net. "These guys crack open coconuts with their claws. After hiding in their burrows all day they've got a lot of nervous energy."

Warning received, I gain a new appreciation for the crab hunters' equipment. The net and tongs, I surmise, must represent a way to neutralize the threat of coconut crab claws.

Eager for the story behind my own presence in the ruins, the crab hunters—who introduce themselves as Ralph and his step-son Milo—listen intently as I recount my encounter with the shark, and subsequent marathon paddle across the lagoon.

"You paddled from Naphali—through that squall?" Ralph marvels. A long whistle through his teeth expresses his thoughts on the matter.

Perhaps moved by the drama of the tale—or more likely, a sense of duty to protect me from further foolishness—Ralph and Milo offer to light my path through the remainder of the ruins and mangrove path. When my famished stomach growls, Ralph and Milo extend their courtesy and invite me to dinner.

"We make coconut crab soup!" Milo says excitedly.

I hesitate to reply, squeamishly eyeing the writhing mass of appendages. Amid the spooky Nan Madol ruins, the creatures appear more monstrous than they might otherwise. Perhaps sensing my hesitation, Ralph asks if I've ever had coconut crab.

"Until now, I'd never heard of coconut crab," I tell him.

"My wife makes amazing coconut crab soup," Ralph says. "People around here consider it quite a treat."

In the end, the longing of my stomach overcomes my hesitation, and I accept the offer. We trace the path out of the swamp, load our eclectic cargo into my sedan, and pile in for what Ralph promises will be a short drive. In the soft glow provided by my car's interior lamp, I get the first real glimpse of my companions. Milo, with a snub nose and bright, eager eyes, looks about ten years old. Ralph, with a receding hairline, salt-and-pepper sideburns, and crow's feet spattered across the corner of his eyes, projects the aura of a weathered explorer who, finding his niche, traded adventure for settled seclusion.

I start the car and drive along a path muddy from the recent rain. Soon, the mangroves part, and a puddle of light, spilled across a welcoming porch, reveals an isolated homestead. As I pull into the driveway, a dog barks. The commotion draws a middle-aged island woman onto the porch, followed by a girl a bit younger than Milo. When Milo brings forth the results of the crab hunt, the women burst into smiles. Ralph gestures for me to follow the group inside.

Worried that my salt-stung eyes and pruned skin — streaked, no doubt, with swamp mud — make me look like a creature dredged from the lagoon, I step hesitantly up to the porch, feeling every bit the awkward guest. However, I soon get a stamp of approval from the family dog, who sniffs my leg and wags its tail. My good character thus affirmed, the family directs me to an outdoor shower, where I wash away my vestiges of awkwardness.

Refreshed from my shower, I retrieve some more presentable clothes from my car. In search of my hosts, I find Ralph sitting quietly on the porch. Awaiting dinner, we sip beers and exchange small talk. Ralph, a biologist doing consultancy work with the Fisheries Department, lives the contented life of a semi-retiree, enjoying the seclusion of Pohnpei's southeast side and the company of his adopted island family. Asking about my life, he learns about my work at the college, and my surf obsession.

"I thought surfers liked Hawaii," he says.

"Well, if surfers knew about waves like those I saw today off Naphali, they'd come in droves. Have you seen anyone else

111

surfing here?"

"Come to think of it, actually I have. A few years back some Australians passed through . . . only, unlike you, they had a boat."

"Oh, I didn't paddle the lagoon by choice," I clarify. "On the outbound journey, I hitched a ride in a bird watcher's skiff."

"A bird watcher?" Ralph asks.

Prodded by Ralph, I recount my experience.

"Sounds like Old Billy," Ralph says. "He lives a short way from here. I've heard he's prone to bouts of drunkenness. But then, he's a 'Nam vet, so I'm not surprised."

"Old Billy, huh? Well, if you see him, tell him I'd like my binoculars back."

Ralph laughs. "Out here, ownership is a fuzzy concept. Consider the coconut crabs. Milo and I caught them, but we don't consider them ours. We share them with the neighbors, who would do the same for us. Old Billy's probably treating your binoculars the same way. And if he was drunk, he might not remember how he got them."

We drain our beers and stare out into the velvet dark beyond the porch lights. Embers of fatigue, reminders of my paddling ordeal, still smolder in my back and arms, but the lamps and kitchen noise of Ralph's homestead convey a domestic comfort. I relax easily, happy to find myself among human company after my solitary combat with the elements. Breathing deep, I inhale the scent of damp soil, and relish the tranquility which settles in the air in the aftermath of a storm. The day's adventures—my ride with the bird watcher, my encounter with the shark, my paddle through the squall, and finally my strange meeting with Ralph and Milo—loop through my mind, and I marvel how my original quest led to an outcome completely unexpected. Could the area's rumored magic have played a role? I ask Ralph if the stories about Nan Madol contain any kernels of truth.

Ralph cracks his knuckles, cracks a smile, and cracks us each another beer. "Superstition pervades these islands," he replies. "Between the fear of witches, the fear of ghosts, and the fear of taboos, it's amazing the locals get anything done." He shakes his head and sighs, seemingly exasperated by a problem long-endured. Then, he slaps me on the shoulder with a strange enthusiasm. "But guess what! Folks like us can bring about change. With our educational backgrounds, we can encourage the islanders to discard their magical beliefs and replace them with critical thinking and the scientific method."

I ponder the benefits such enlightenment would bring to my classroom endeavors.

"As for Nan Madol—well, hopefully the islanders would learn to regard the ruins scientifically," Ralph says. "They'd apply Occam's Razor—the idea that the simplest explanation is the likeliest—and realize the absurdity of thinking that strange lights in the ruins represent the ghosts of Micronesian sorcerers."

"So, you never see strange lights in the ruins?"

"Oh sure. I've seen strange lights floating through from time to time. I just don't think they're ghosts."

"What are they?"

"Probably trans-dimensional spacecraft."

Ralph stares long and thoughtfully into the night, and in the unnerving silence that envelopes us, I wonder if he's joking or serious.

"Whoever built Nan Madol employed a technology beyond our comprehension," Ralph explains. "I wouldn't give much credence to ghost stories. Anyone with half a brain and a background in critical thinking can look at the evidence and see that UFOs, not Micronesian sorcerers, explain the mystery of Nan Madol."

*   *   *

Excerpt from a Diary, September 1999:

In line for the bar at Club Flamingo, I meet her, the Japanese girl with the jasmine perfume. She wears stiletto heels and a jade pendant that invites a glance toward her neckline. Apart from her nose, of an aquiline variety slightly too large for her face, she exudes a refined beauty, a blend of Western style and Eastern mystique, and from the way a table of elder ex-pats eyes her, I can tell her effect extends through the room. Seeing the empty glass in her hand, I offer to buy her a drink.

"Oh, you genterman!" she says, her accent transforming l to r. "From time I first see you, I know you genterman."

"Well, I try," I say. "What's your poison?"

"Po-san?"

"What would you like to drink?"

"Oh. I rike Bruddy Mary!"

Together, we sidle up to the bar, and wait for the bartender to finish his prior orders. As we wait, we exchange names. She leans toward my ear. "You my kind of man," she whispers.

Eventually, I place the order, but get bad news: no Bloody Mary mix. The bartender advises us to visit the Village Hotel, purveyors of the best Bloody Marys on the island, all from fresh ingredients. The recommendation excites Akane, who coyly transforms my drink offer into a dinner date.

Though beyond my budget and a bit of a drive, the Village Hotel promises a romantic setting, and I acquiesce, lured by Akane's petite figure and flattering comments.

Once at the hotel, I feel more like a charlatan than a gentleman. Our table in the dining area places us alongside the upper-echelons of island visitors: retirees on round-the-world trips, businessmen seeking deals with island moguls, and perhaps a few diplomatic types mingling with representatives from the FSM legislature—in short, people who

114

spend in a day what I earn in a month. Then, remembering the credit card in my wallet, I settle more easily in my chair, order two Bloody Marys, and pretend not to notice when Akane orders the most expensive dish on the menu.

"You my kind of man," Akane tells me again, when the waiter departs. "You treat girl right." Her smile, engineered for flattery, could make even the most committed cheapskate abandon his budget.

But later, when the dinner arrives, I find Akane strangely changed. Instead of flattery, I now only hear the clink of silverware. The glances that she once reserved for me she now directs only to her plate. And, later that night, after I pay the bill and drive her back to town—a drive which she seems to endure in awkward discomfort—my goodbye kiss meets only a grudgingly-presented cheek.

A week later, during a gathering at the Australian embassy, I see her by the pool, an empty cocktail glass in hand. She pretends not to recognize me, instead reserving her attention for a dapper young member of the embassy staff. Seeing her empty glass, he offers to get her a drink.

"Oh, you genterman!" I hear her tell him. "You my kind of man."

Chapter 6: Traveler's Tales

The *Iris*, fifty feet of fiberglass hull decked with sun-baked teak, floats with sails close-furled, ignoring the zephyrs that swirl by its mast. Nearby, at anchor or tied to mooring buoys, other sailboats assume a similar languid repose, awaiting the return of crews for whom Pohnpei, like a garden oasis in an ocean desert, provides an alluring interruption to a trans-Pacific voyage.

For the *Iris*, in need of repairs to its marine diesel engine, Pohnpei's harbor represents a necessary pit stop for repairs. Henrik, the 28-year old captain, piratical with a swarthy beard and red bandanna, regards the mechanical matter as an excuse to linger long near the Rumours Bar, exercising his appetite for cold beer and ex-pat conversation. Recognizing Henrik as a wave-rider full of traveler's tales, I take a seat at his table. Always eager to give new arrivals a lesson in international relations, Lana, the Australian Volunteer, does likewise. Beer in hand, a map of the Western Pacific spread upon the table, Henrik recalls the circumstances that left him marooned in one of Micronesia's backwater bars.

Henrik's journey began when he helped crew the *Iris* from San Diego to Australia, where the boat's owner—a real estate developer with a variety of holdings—departed after completing a leisurely trans-Pacific cruise. Called to Hawaii on business, the developer left Henrik in charge of crew and delivering the *Iris* to Honolulu. Regarding the assignment as an open-ended invitation to chase swell and probe paradise, Henrik summoned a crew of fellow Californians, surf pirates all, who flew to meet him with a mantra of "adventure first, boat-delivery second" in mind.

After a few weeks of preparation, they sailed the *Iris* out of Australia, departing Sydney harbor as the forepaws of a Southern Hemisphere winter swiped at their stern. They spent some weeks cruising off Brisbane and the northern Gold Coast, swerved around the Great Barrier Reef, set a course north through the Coral Sea, and dropped anchor off the Solomon Islands, where they enjoyed two months of waves and wandering. With the Southern Hemisphere swell season on the wane, they set their prow on another northward track, crossing the equator toward

Micronesia. Near the end of the passage, one of the crew developed a stomach ailment. In their haste to reach medical care, they augmented their sails by running the diesel a little too hard, ignored the warnings of the temperature gauge, and added an overheated engine to their worries. In need of repair to body and boat, they arrived in Pohnpei in early October, just as the trade winds began a seasonal switch from southwest to northeast. The sick crew member, diagnosed with food poisoning, began a recovery after a few days of hospital-administered I.V. fluids. The marine diesel, diagnosed with a blown head gasket, required a parts shipment that could take months to materialize, or so the mechanic at Kolonia Marine Supply told them.

For a group of surf pirates used to wandering the wind, the immobility proved maddening, and one by one they returned to their old lives, bequeathing the *Iris* an eclectic detritus: a half-dozen surfboards in padded travel bags, sprinkled with spare leashes, fins and bars of wax; a bongo drum and two acoustic guitars, left propped against the lifeboat; diving masks, snorkels, and swim-fins, heaped under the boom. A California beach party in sailboat guise, the *Iris* reflects a romantic, live-for-the-moment lifestyle, whose thrills Henrik summarizes with pithy nostalgia: "We had a good time."

"Awesome," I say. "I've always wanted to do a sailboat surfari."

Lana rolls her eyes, as if Henrik's tale makes melodrama of a quotidian quest. "Sounds boring," she says. "Definitely not my cup of tea."

"That's because you don't surf," I retort. "Most surfers would relish the idea of a sailboat surf trip."

"Most surfers are idiots," Lana asserts.

"That's a harsh assessment," I say, hearing in Lana's words an insult in need of rebuke, or at least a logical fallacy worthy of critique. Henrik raises his eyebrows.

119

Lana shrugs, unapologetic. "I'm from Australia. I've dated plenty of surfers, and they care only about one thing."

"What's that?" Henrik and I ask, anticipating some further slight to our sub-culture.

"Material pleasure," Lana pronounces.

"You say it like it's a bad thing," Henrik says, beer bottle at his lips.

"It's childish, selfish, and produces only false happiness," Lana admonishes. "It is a bad thing."

"False happiness!" I chortle. "Let me tell you what it's like to ride a wave. . ."

"Oh, let me guess," Lana interjects, her voice full of derision. "It's like flying! It's a moment of pure instinct, in which you merge with the elements! When you ride the tube, time stands still! Blah blah blah. . .boring."

"Surfers don't think it's boring," I say, somewhat lamely.

"That's because most surfers are idiots," Lana says, dismissing my retort with a smug smile.

I glance at Henrik, seeking an alliance against Lana's logic, but Henrik simply grins, nursing his beer.

"False happiness only brings discontent," Lana continues. "If we want true happiness, we must abandon the pursuit of material pleasure, and help solve the world's problems."

"How do we do that?" Henrik asks, in the cynical tone of a world traveler well-versed in the various forms of spiritual salesmanship.

"I joined the Australian Volunteers," Lana says. "Your path my take a different course. But all paths share a main feature: a selfless dedication to improving the lives of others."

"Well, I'm a teacher," I respond. "That's gotta count for something."

"You get a paycheck," Lana retorts. "That's a job, not

selfless dedication."

"Try reading some of the essays I have to grade. Then we'll talk about dedication."

"Cute," Lana smirks. "But when you finish grading papers, you pursue the material pleasure known as surfing. Meanwhile, the real problems of the island go unaddressed. For example, did you know that Micronesia has an abnormally high rate of teen depression and suicide?

"I did hear something about that," Henrik says, elbows propped on the table. "Something about clan culture and the psychological oppression it creates?"

"Right," Lana says, nodding in appreciation of Henrik's familiarity with the issue. "Island youth grow up in an extended family structure that deprives them of anonymity and magnifies any embarrassment. That, combined with the claustrophobic confines of island geography, sometimes makes suicide seem like the only form of escape."

"That's why education is so important," I say, in praise of the professoriate. "College will help students explore their options in a wider world, so they don't have to let clan culture define them."

"How many island kids actually go to college?" Lana questions. "COM-FSM serves only a small percent of the population. You need to get involved beyond the college if you want to make a difference."

"I'm an English teacher, not Mother Theresa," I reply defensively.

"There are other ways, besides the classroom, to provide service," Lana clarifies. "What this island could really use is more political activism. Do you realize that U.S. corporations play a major role in the surge of obesity and heart disease among Micronesians?"

"U.S. corporations?" I ask, anticipating an anti-American

121

rant for which Henrik and I no doubt represent convenient proxy-targets.

"Yes, U.S. corporations," Lana reiterates. "You Americans won't eat turkey tails, so American food industry exports them to the Pacific islands. High in fat and low in cost, they've become a staple at local gatherings, especially funeral feasts, which in clan culture take place once or twice a month. The more islanders go to funerals, the more they eat turkey tails, which in turn only lead to more funerals. It's a vicious cycle."

"Circle," I amend, correcting her pronunciation. "The proper phrase is 'vicious circle.'"

"Excuse me?"

"You pronounced the vowel long, as in 'cycle.' But 'circle' doesn't have a long vowel."

"You're a real jerk, you know that?"

Her accent deletes the post-vocalic "r", making "jerk" sound like "jack."

"I think you mean 'jerk,'" I say, emphasizing the post-vocalic 'r.'

Irritated, Lana heads off to the bathroom.

"She's interesting," Henrik says. "Do you know much about her? She has an earthy sort of energy."

"She brought a platter of pot brownies to my door when I first arrived on the island. I had an unpleasant reaction to them. Since then, I've been avoiding her."

"She's kinda cute. . . in an earthy sort of way," Henrik opines. "Did you notice the skimpy bikini beneath her blouse?"

"No."

In truth, I do notice, Lana's earthy beauty being a well-known topic among lovelorn expats. Lithe, blonde, and possessed of a shameless fashion sense which seems designed to intentionally provoke the male imagination, Lana provides a target for many a passionate plot. Her ability to keep aspiring suitors at a disdainful distance only adds to the intrigue. Despite the brownie incident, I find myself charmed by her spell, and only by pretending otherwise do I avoid acting like a fool in her presence.

Henrik stands, stretches, and shuffles over to the pool table, where he lackadaisically pots the balls left over from a prior game. I watch his cue-craft and sip my beer. As I bring the bottle to my lips, a tap on my shoulder turns my attention to a little waif of a girl, her dirt-sullied skirt and T-shirt smelling of mud and mangrove. Her face, of a forlorn variety that only a Scrooge could ignore, fixes me in a desperate gaze that drips pathos upon a wooden trinket clutched in her hands.

"Sir, you like shark carving? Please sir! I sell for ten dollars."

Instead of the cheap and gaudy tourist trash I expect, the carving possesses a subtle elegance, with exquisite lines and shell-inlay eyes. Seeing in the shark a bit of memorabilia that could double as a paper weight for my office desk, I decide to purchase the trinket, and dig a 20-dollar bill from my wallet.

"Wait here while I break this twenty," I tell the girl. Money in hand, I rise from my chair, intending to obtain change at the bar. As I do, the alarmed voice of Marleen, the zaftig and usually doe-eyed barmaid, blares through the air.

"Shoo! Get out, you little rat!" she yells at the waif. "Stay away from bar! No bother customer!"

With my attention suddenly turned to Marleen, the waif plucks the money from my fingers and scampers outside, leaving the shark carving on the table.

"Sorry sir," the barmaid says, on a mission of damage control. Scanning the premises, she searches for any further sign of the waif. "I not see her come in."

Lana, back from the bathroom, asks about the ruckus.

"Oh, no worries," I say, in stoic contemplation of the

incident. "I guess I'm now the proud owner of that trinket."

"This not trinket!" the barmaid announces, tracing a finger along the carving's burnished surface. "This Kapingan wish charm. Very powerful." She places the carving back on the table, as if fearing to hold it longer.

"A Kapingan wish charm?" I ask.

"I think the fishermen use them," Lana puts in. "They place the carving in the sea as an offering, to ensure a good catch. Interesting. . .I've never actually seen one."

"I'm not very fond of fishing," I say.

"You don't have to wish for fish," the barmaid says. "You can wish for money. . . women. . .even a change in the weather."

"No kidding?"

"One year, when I little girl, no rain come," the barmaid recollects. "My family try to grow yams, but yams not grow. So, my uncle took wish charm up Sokeh's Ridge and wish for rain. Next day, rains come!"

"Why did your uncle go to Sokeh's Ridge? Is that a special place?" I ask.

"Because it's close to the clouds," she explains, exasperated by my ignorance of wish charms and their manner of operation. "If you ask something of the clouds, you have to get close to where they can hear you." Shaking her head, she ambles back to the bar.

"Sokeh's is supposed to be the energy center of the island," Lana says. "I've been up there, and it does feel a bit strange. According to legend, the Saudeleurs used basalt quarried from Sokeh's in the construction of Nan Madol." She looks at the wish charm thoughtfully. Perhaps inspired by its possible uses, she suggests an altruistic adventure: a hike up Sokeh's Ridge, from whose rarefied ramparts the power of the wish charm can diffuse across the island.

"What should we wish for?" Henrik asks. "A ban on

turkey tails?"

"Not a bad idea," Lana grins. "We'll think of something."

Intrigued more by the prospect of an afternoon with Lana than by credence in the wish charm, I join the expedition, motivated, additionally, by the chance that I might encounter the waif and extract my ten dollars of change.

Henrik takes a minute to grab some gear from his boat, and returns with pocket binoculars, bug repellent, and bottled water. Wish charm in hand, Lana leads, and we emerge from the bar, blinking like mid-day moviegoers whose eyes, unused to daylight, require a moment of readjustment. Almost immediately, our altruistic adventure confronts conflict. By an overstuffed trash bin, a sudden outburst of barks, growls, and yelps signals a dogfight, from which the loser, a ragged mutt whose rib bones protrude along its muddy flanks, backs slowly away to curl up and lick its wounds. One head gash, evidently from a prior fight and now infected so the swelling lifts the fur away from the bone, reveals brief glimpses of the dog's skull. A grisly portrait of the world's random cruelty, the sight helps galvanize Lana's resolve. "The island needs our help," she says.

In search of the trailhead, Lana leads us through a ramshackle neighborhood of cement houses whose back walls line the base of Sokeh's Ridge. The air, of a greasy quality redolent of slow-cooked pig, sticks in our throats. As we approach a yard full of laundry on clotheslines, small children, their faces masked with mischief, poke their heads between the edges of hanging sheets and wag their tongues. Henrik offers a friendly wave. In return we get a pebble barrage, intended more to irritate than injure, though some of the well-hurled irritants sting our legs like horseflies. Positioned now on the edge of the yard, the children add a verbal component to the physical hostility, filling our ears with insults.

"Hey mehnwei!" one child taunts. "God must not like

you. . . he made you so ugly!"

"Ugly! Ugly! Ugly!" the others chant. "Why God make you ugly?"

"Hey mehnwei!" another jeers. "Does God hate you? He made you so stinky!"

"Stinky! Stinky! Stinky!" they chant in unison. "Why God make you stinky?"

As we move beyond pebble range, the vicious verses culminate in a rude refrain: "Fook you mehnwei! Fook you mehnwei! Foooook yoooooouuu!"

Coming from the mouths of babes, the vitriol carries a perplexing punch, which we tolerate with the help of Lana's sociological insights.

"Just ignore them," she advises. "To these kids, foreigners are like stray dogs, lacking the protection of an extended family network. So, they test behavioral boundaries, certain that clan culture will insulate them from meaningful retaliation."

"Someday they might push the boundaries with the wrong person," I say. "Clan culture might not provide as much protection as they think."

"Maybe we should wish for the kids to learn some manners," Henrik suggests.

"We need to wish for a lot of things," Lana mutters.

A gap appears between homes, and we spy a trailhead, protruding like a gravelly toe from the forested foot of the ridge. Along the edges of the trail, ferns, vines, and densely-packed hardwoods tangle in a bushy brawl. Seen in the pages of *National Geographic*, such a landscape might inspire armchair travelers to adventurous ambition, questing for ancient ruins down a machete-hewn path. Seen in person, with the rich aroma of blossoming plants and rotting leaves, the screech of birds and the drone of bugs, the scene inspires more caution. Beyond the sunlit foliage of the trailhead, shadow-ensconced trees stand guard, I imagine, over ravines of perpetual darkness, where the eyes of forest creatures resemble pale lamps suspended in the gloom.

Led by Lana, we ignore the menace of the trees, and follow the trail along ascending switchbacks where the heat of the day, trapped by a canopy of leaves, broods with malevolence. We find a break in the forest, but not in our perspiration, as we traverse a black volcanic cliff and angle toward the ridge crest. The trail makes a final series of switchbacks to the top, flattens out, and enters a hall of trees extending along the line of the ridge. Amid the trees, thickets of bamboo sway and clatter. Two scents, one of decayed roots and moist soil, the other of vibrant leaves charged with sunlight, form a primal atmosphere, where the anomalous remains of a Japanese anti-aircraft gun provide a rusting footprint of humanity's prior intrusions.

Despite a growth of lichen along its barrels, and a calligraphy of vines among its turret gears, the gun retains a sinister air, its wicked symmetry undiminished by time. The whisper of wind among the trees adds a spooky mood, making the gun seem like a trysting place for the Pacific War's lost ghosts. With my gaze aimed along the barrels, I imagine peering back through more than half a century into a World War Two panorama, where Japanese soldiers scan the skies for American planes, Pohnpeian laborers slavishly haul supplies up the ridge trail, and a naval vessel, at anchor in the harbor, hoists the Flag of the Rising Sun. A twig snaps, and the vision fades; in its place comes the sight of Henrik, stooping to pluck a shiny object from the carpet of leaves.

"I doubt the Japanese left this," Henrik says, brushing soil from the soda can, its faded green and white 7-Up logo still recognizable. He places the can atop one of the gun's turret gears. For some reason, the juxtaposition of the can and the gun creates a strange aesthetic, robbing the gun of its majesty. What at first

*WWII relic, one of several rusting in the jungle atop Sokeh's Ridge.
The islands of Micronesia, particularly the Western Micronesian
islands of Chuuk and Palau, offer a treasure trove for WWII buffs.
Wary of Pohnpei's difficult terrain and heavy rainfall, the U.S.
military opted to bypass the island in its westward drive across the
Pacific during WWII. In some parts of Micronesia, sale of scrap
metal from WWII relics provides an income source for enterprising
islanders.*

impressed me as a stately relic now seems like another bit of trash, providing only a cynical statement about the fate of the works of man. Turning away, we continue down the hall of trees.

The trail follows the backbone of the ridge, its leaf-carpeted surface dotted now and again by muddy puddles which spew mosquitoes at our approach. We brush past a final thicket of vines and come to a grassy precipice where the foliage gives way to plunging cliffs and a close-up view of Sokeh's Rock, whose basaltic cranium bisects our view of the horizon. Apparently lofted by the landscape to an atmosphere of less inhibition, Lana strips down to her bikini, reclines upon the grass, and places the shark carving on her chest, granting its shell-inlay eyes a view sought unsuccessfully by many a suitor.

Struggling mightily to maintain my pretense of disinterest, I ignore the Aphroditic apparition exemplified by Lana's supine figure, borrow Henrik's pocket binoculars, and distract myself with a survey of the surroundings. In the lagoon below, an assortment of reefs mottles the water like red-brown amoebas in a petri dish. Focusing on Kolonia's harbor front, I observe a freighter, its bilge spewing caramel-colored effluent. On the wharf, a trash fire, tended by the matchstick figures of dockworkers, billows a pall of black smoke. Much like the remains of the anti-aircraft gun, the sight prods me to dark reflections. In hopes of a contrast, I turn toward the barrier reefs bordering the open ocean, and discern, counter-clockwise from east to west, a series of reef passes, their waters azure and sparkling, their tapering edges perfect receivers for whatever swell the Northwest Pacific might churn up. Untainted by septic scenes, cruel kids, or rotting relics, the reef passes comprise a playground of purity, and hope fills my heart.

"Wow," I say, mesmerized momentarily by something other than Lana. "Those reef passes must get epic!"

"If you believe the rumors," Henrik says, grabbing the

Looking North toward the parietal portion of Sokeh's Rock's basaltic cranium, with the tapering edges of the reef at Main Pass visible in the background. Also known as the "Diamond Head of Micronesia," the landmark serves as a navigational aid for ships approaching Pohnpei's harbor.

pocket binoculars for a look of his own.

"Rumors?" I inquire.

"Well, more like guarded stories," he amends. "An acquaintance, who works on a charter boat back home, spent a few years in Micronesia during the late 80's. He used to tell us that Pohnpei had an amazing right that broke along a reef pass located west of the harbor. Palikir, he called it. I think he meant that one yonder," Henrik says, pointing west.

"A perfect reef pass, waiting for a perfect swell" I muse. "Maybe the wish charm can help."

"I won't waste energy catering to your frivolous pursuits," Lana admonishes. Seated now in lotus position, she clasps both hands to the wish charm, and holds it out toward Sokeh's rock. Inhaling deeply, perhaps savoring an atmosphere only she can appreciate, Lana closes her eyes and leaves us to our surf talk.

"I bet a lot of these reef passes have their day," I opine. "They just require the right combination of swell and wind."

"Well, I used to feel optimistic," Henrik sighs. "But I've sailed through a big chunk of the Pacific. After investigating hundreds of islands and countless reefs, I've concluded that good waves are a rarity. A lot of spots look promising to the eye, or on a nautical chart, but reveal major flaws once a swell arrives. An A-frame peak may turn to a dry reef suck-out, or a juicy wall may fizzle as it suddenly hits deep water. Without swell, you just can't tell."

"No swell, no tell," I murmur, appreciating the pithy truth in Henrik's words.

"My guess," Henrik says, scanning the reef passes, "is that the Northeast trade wind, once it starts, blows chop into most of these spots. You'd need a break with western exposure, so the trade wind blows from an off-shore angle."

Turning the binoculars westward, we glass the line of

reefs, our demeanor like that of pilgrims who, after a long journey, regard from a distance the fabled architecture of a long-sought temple.

"You'll never find a perfect wave" Lana states, emerging from her meditation.

The statement rattles our rapture, but Henrik offers an optimistic reply. "Though rare, perfect wavs definitely exist," he says. "Finding them just requires patience and dedication."

"The problem is the human ability to experience perfection," Lana replies. "Unless you have cultivated perfection within yourself, you won't find it in the world outside."

"Maybe the pursuit of external perfection helps cultivate an internal awareness," I posit, clamoring for a share of Lana's attention. "Consider the possibility that riding a wave is a meditative act, through which our bodies, consisting mostly of water, flow in harmony with the ancient brine of the sea, the origin of life. The better the wave, the more transcendent the connection. Perhaps surfing perfect waves provides a gateway to our true selves." I think I've scored a point, but Lana seems unimpressed.

"Material pleasure can never create a connection with our true selves," Lana rebukes. "For the sake of argument, however, let's put your hypothesis to the test. Tell me, how many good waves have you ridden?"

"Plenty," I say, as twenty years' worth of surfing memories come to mind. "Hundreds."

"In that case, according to your hypothesis, you should be well on your way to transcendence. . . correct?"

"I guess so," I say, agreeing with Lana's logic even as I chafe at the scrutiny of my spirit.

Lana smiles. "Now tell me--what do you see when you look at me?"

The question functions as an invitation, and I let the full

force of Lana's earthy attraction fill my gaze. From the floodgates of desire long repressed, I release an answer. "A hot blond in a bikini!" I exclaim with a grin.

"If you were in touch with your true self, you would see a being of light, whose aura glows green at the edges." Sighing with exasperation, she gathers her things and struts toward the trail.

"Where are you going?" I blurt, desperate for some sign that the attraction might be mutual.

"Someplace where I don't have to deal with your mindset of material pleasure," she says. "Associating with people who don't understand my energy only inhibits my growth."

Dismissively, she tosses the wish charm on the grass, her policy of non-association extending, apparently, even to material objects to which I might stake a claim.

That evening, sunset hues drip from the sky into the lagoon, painting watercolors of amber orange around the silhouette of the *Iris*. Beers in hand, Henrik and I sit at the deck of the Rumours Bar and admire the vista. The stereo behind the bar serenades us and a few other patrons with synthesizer-driven techno. In an interlude between songs, Henrik asks me what I intend to do with the wish charm.

"Originally, I bought it as a paper-weight for my office desk," I say.

"It makes a nice souvenir," Henrik says. "Of course, if you keep it as a souvenir, you won't know its true potential."

"Don't tell me you actually believe this wish charm stuff," I say.

"Aren't you a little bit curious?" Henrik replies.

I turn the carving around in my hands and ponder its contours. As the shell-inlay eyes gleam back at me, my sentiments shift. What before seemed exquisite now seems accusatory, a reminder of Lana's rebuke at the ridge. Knowing the shark will only make me re-live that moment, I decide Henrik has a point.

I rise from the table, meander to where the bar's outdoor deck extends on stilts into the lagoon, and cast the carving into the water.

"What did you wish for?" Henrik asks, after I return to the table.

"Some waves," I say. "Some really good waves."

"Sweet," Henrik says. Applauding my choice, he raises a toast to "material pleasure."

Seeing us drain our beers, the barmaid approaches. "More cold ones?" she asks.

Henrik nods.

"How come Lana not with you?" she wonders.

"She got mad and left us," Henrik says.

"Why she got mad?"

"Jacques can't see her aura," Henrik explains, chuckling.

"Oh," the barmaid ponders, a look of confusion crossing her face. "Well, if you need girlfriend, just call my sister. She lets you see everything!"

Excerpt from a Diary, October 1999:

With the College closed in observance of United Nations' Day, a holiday which generates little interest in the U.S. but occasions fanfare in this developing island outpost, I find Kolonia abuzz with a celebratory atmosphere, an inspiration, at least momentarily, to put aside personal interest and reflect on one's contribution to the global community. True to my materialistic American heritage, I ignore such higher purpose, and instead drive to the harbor offices of Pohnpei Transfer and Storage, whose management, some days prior, sent notice to the College that my shipping container from Los Angeles had arrived and "would I please complete the proper paperwork, otherwise P T&S could pay fees for keeping the container in a warehouse."

Eager to claim my property, I reconnoiter the waterfront, searching for the P T&S sign. As I do, a maritime montage rolls past my driver's side window. Aboard a Chinese fishing junk, which smells of bilge water and diesel, a crew clad in stained khakis dangle cigarettes from their mouths and regard me with a curious mixture of envy and hate, as though the sight of me and my rattletrap sedan represents a fantasy life they envision with jealousy. Further along, by a concrete wharf padded with tires, the listing hulk of an old passenger ferry succumbs to neglect, its deck cabins and hull and amalgam of blistered paint, barnacles, and rust. Finally, the P T&S sign looms above a dirt lot, where an obstacle course of freight-related detritus—palette jacks with missing handles, splintered pieces of shipping crates, and cast-off bits of old appliances—forces me to weave a circuitous path to the reception area. Once at the reception counter, I find the Pohnpeian version of Bluto, chest and forearms bulging across the countertop. His greeting, a greasy smile more conniving than congenial, suggests my arrival represents the possibility of some underhanded transaction.

"Hi," I say, my voice serrated with a guttural edge that I

135

imagine appropriate for dockside dealings. "I received notice that a freight shipment arrived for me?"

"Name?"

"Jacques. I teach at the College."

"Oh, you teach at the COLLEGE," he says, feigning awe. "What sort of freight you got?"

"I've got furniture, computer equipment, cookware, a guitar, and. . . I'm not sure why it's any of your business," I remark, suddenly suspicious.

"Not my business?" he says, greasy smile turning toothsome. "Ever hear of something called a Bill of Lading? The Customs Office wants to know the value of your goods."

"Why do they care about that?"

"So they can charge a value tax," he says, drawing out the pronunciation of "tax" as if to add emphasis to unpleasant information. "After you pay value tax, Customs Office give you stamp, which I match to Bill of Lading."

"Where's the Customs Office?"

"Next to the State Tax Office," he says. "You gotta go there afterward."

"The State Tax Office? Why do I have to go there?"

"To pay a Use Tax," he grins, beady eyes dancing with merriment at the disconcerting effect these revelations have on me. "The Use Tax is based on the Value Tax."

"How much will it be?" I squeak, my voice now that of a country mouse chastened by the complexities of customs policy. My eagerness to retrieve my property founders on the fear that I can't afford to claim it.

"Mebbe a couple hundred dollars," he says. "The sooner you process your paperwork, the less chance you pay extra fees at this end."

"Anything else I should know?" I ask, discomfited by the Kafka-esque bureaucracy I apparently must navigate.

"You American?" he asks, pushing his elbows to the edge of the

counter, a location particularly promotional to his forearm bulk. I have no doubt that in his youth he was the type of character who tortured small animals and bullied the neighborhood youth—a personality trait he perhaps never outgrew.

"Yes," I nod.

"I don't like Americans."

Harbor region overview, as seen from the trail ascending Sokeh's Ridge, from which shadows extend into the left foreground. Much of the funding for dock facilities, airport improvements, and other expensive infrastructure came to the FSM courtesy of the U.S. as part of a Compact of Free Association. Between freighter arrivals, which heralded an infusion of goods to Kolonia's retail establishments, the harbor basked in an atmosphere of lazy torpor.

As with much in politics, the Compact of Free Association had critics, who contended that providing funds for expensive infrastructure only perpetuated a need for more funds, since the FSM economy, on its own, could not generate the revenue necessary for infrastructure maintenance. To the extent that the Compact also helped fund education, and in turn my paycheck from the College, my feelings on the matter weren't entirely agnostic.

Wish charm magic? Fabulous lefts create a goofy-footer's dream, Main Pass, October 1999. In October, as the Intertropical Convergence Zone followed the sun south toward the Austral summer, days of light air combined with proto-swell from the North Pacific, and sections of reef that rarely showed good form might suddenly turn on. Peeling along the shallows that comprise the western edge of Main Pass, these lefts made for a novelty, but set waves were shifting, inconsistent, and maddeningly difficult to gauge.

Chapter 7: Sips from the Chalice of Neptune

Riley Schroff pans his gaze around the Rumours Bar, sizing up the crowd. With worldly wisdom, he informs me that the sad-sack story of my broken engagement will only play like a broken record among the hardcore guzzlers who flank our position, their tables bristling with "brain grenades"—Riley's military-minded appellation for drinks. With the proper attitude adjustment, he suggests, I might gain an appreciation for island charms, and discard the emotional baggage associated with my ex- fiancée.

Presenting a dossier of scintillating stories about ex-pat life, Riley establishes his credentials as a well-equipped waterman, replete with boat (a 17-foot Carolina Skiff), an assortment of waterman's gear (ranging from fishing equipment to sailboards and surfboards), and various other possessions befitting someone who enjoys a lucrative gig as a helicopter pilot for the purse seiner fleet. Originally from North Carolina, where he flew charters after leaving the military, he finds amusement in my California slang, while I find amusement in the occasional samples of military parlance that color his conversation. Over beer and an occasional game of pool, we indulge in mainland memories, though Riley does so with a bitterness that contrasts with my nostalgia.

"At least here I don't get grounded by red tape and regulations," Riley tells me, gritting his teeth. His eyes, lady-killer cuts of topaz infused with blue curacao, turn icy. "Do you know the rigamarole required to keep a helo charter within FAA operational compliance?" Not waiting for an answer, he reproduces his version of the experience. "Whoosh! whoosh!" he mimes. "That's the sound of government fees sucking away your profits." Indignant with the memory, Riley takes a lengthy draught of beer.

Thinking that some surf talk might pave the way to more favorable common ground, I recall my adventures along the island's Southeast side, including my shark encounter at Naphali. Riley listens with a bemused smile, the way a seasoned sport-fisherman might listen to a neophyte angler talk about catching trout.

"I think you need to develop your sense of target discrimination," he teases as I pause to swig my beer. "That place

142

is low on amps and voltage. I don't even bother with it."

"Low on amps and voltage?" I question, convinced the waves at Naphali would draw a sizeable crowd in California.

"The real wave is Palikir Pass," he tells me, lowering his voice a notch. "Surf season hasn't really started yet."

"Palikir?" I reply, recalling prior rumors about a wave to the west of the harbor. "What's it like?"

Leaning across the table, Riley wraps his words in whisper. "World class," he states. "Like nothing you've surfed before."

Riley settles back in his seat, studying the intrigued expression that no doubt characterizes my face. The phrase "world class" rattles around my skull like a shiny coin, and my mind spools through an honor roll of famous spots—Honolua Bay, Rincon, Uluwatu, etc.--that, in surf lore, merit such billing. Warily, I ponder the many surfers who gravitate to such spots.

"What about crowds?" I ask, my voice full of foreboding.

The corners of Riley's lips curl into a smile. "Just you and me," he says.

The idea of a world-class wave breaking in secrecy defies belief. "Don't surfers travel here for it?" I question, voicing my doubts. "After all, *Surfer* magazine recently issued a travel report for this region."

"A few solo travelers come out here," he affirms. "Last winter a guy from Guam shared a few sessions with me. But, they don't live here. We do. As for the travel report—well, let's just say it contains some glaring inaccuracies. I wonder if the people who compiled it really did their recon."

"I see."

"The average traveler stands a good chance of getting skunked here. The surf can go flat for weeks on end. The northeast trade winds make for choppy conditions at most spots. The weather can turn outright depressing. Over the years, this island likely played host to various surf travelers who arrived, looked, and left without ever knowing a dream wave slumbered offshore, waiting for the right moment to awaken."

Outside, the velvet curtain of a tropical night hangs over the deck and billows in through the door. Riley drains his bottle and succumbs to a yawn.

"I've had a long week," he says. "Maybe tomorrow we can take the boat out for a spin, do some fishing. Have you ever snorkeled a reef pass? From underwater, you can glean Palikir's potential for perfection. Also, I can introduce you to the sharks," he says, chuckling softly.

"Sounds good, except for the sharks," I say

The next morning, I follow directions to a waterfront neighborhood where single-story houses, yards blooming with boating paraphernalia, reflect their maritime-minded residents. Though the directions help me find Riley's house, they mention nothing about the two dogs who snarl at me as I approach the front door. Startled, I cower while the dogs ring me in a barking circle of fur, fangs, and frothy saliva.

"That's my Stink Bomb!" comes a voice of praise through the din. "That's my Fitty Cal!" Riley steps out to the porch and claps his hands. Tails a-wag in celebration of their successful mock attack, the dogs trot over to the porch. Beaming like a proud parent, Riley hands them each a treat.

"I've been training them for guard duty," he explains. "Being half wild, they tend to get a bit aggressive." Based on the enthusiasm with which he says this, I infer that he views such a tendency as something to cultivate.

Invited inside, I step through the doorway and survey a spacious living room, where a set of comfortable sofas face a wide-screen T.V., its screen commanding an audience of beer cans, peanut shells, and pretzels assembled on a coffee table. On a wall to the right of the doorway hangs a poster-size photograph of a flawless, large, un-ridden wave looking very much the equal to anything depicted in magazines. As I admire the photo, Riley places a videocassette of *Apocalypse Now* in the VCR. Soon, the bold refrain of "Ride of the Valkyries," from the movie's famous helicopter assault scene, blares from the T.V., lending our excursion an element of ceremonial fanfare. Flutes flourish as Riley hands me a plastic tub of snorkeling gear; bassoons boom as he loads fishing equipment, including hooks, lures, and trolling lines; and trombones triumph as he brings forth beer in an ice chest. Proclaiming us "operationally mobile," Riley hitches his truck to the boat trailer, fills the dogs' food and water bowls, and starts the truck.

A brief drive leads us to the airport causeway and a clearing among the mangroves. At the edge of the clearing, rutted tracks lead toward the lagoon. We back the boat trailer down the tracks and stop when the lagoon water laps along the hull of the Carolina Skiff. Stepping out of the truck, Riley instructs me to hold the boat in place while he releases it from the trailer. I wade in to the water and grab the bow railing, resisting a subtle yet insistent current that drags the boat laterally along the causeway shore. I shuffle my feet for better leverage, and in the process drive a piece of coral rubble into my heel. When Riley clambers into the boat and fiddles with some knobs on the center console, I interpret the moment as a signal to come aboard. I sit down on the deck and dig the offending coral from my foot, only to have an excoriating voice assault my ear.

"What are you doing?" Riley scolds, his demeanor that of a captain berating a deckhand. "Do you realize you've cast the boat adrift before I've verified the operational status of the engine?"

Surprised, I stammer a few words about the coral rubble, and gesture toward the causeway shore, which lies peacefully perhaps five feet from our bow.

"Proximity to land does not give one an excuse to discard the rules of seamanship," Riley says with authority. "Even on a calm day, a boater places himself in implacable forces. Never put to sea without establishing confidence in the seaworthiness of your craft!" he warns, evaluating my maritime acumen and not liking what he sees.

More calmly, he continues, a commander briefing his subordinate: "I've outfitted this boat in full battle-rattle. In the chest, you'll find a flare gun; on the console, a GPS navigation aid; and, under the console, an EPIRB, capable of creating an emergency radio signal. While we're downrange, I don't want any smoking and joking."

Lecture complete, he grabs a Miller Lite from the ice chest, takes a long guzzle, and toggles a switch on the center console. The outboard sputters to life and soon we glide at about 15 knots across the lagoon and into the shipping channel, the skiff's bow chattering over the tops of glittering wavelets. Dominating the vista to our left, Sokeh's rock thrusts skyward, its basaltic countenance darkly reflected upon the lagoon's surface. We motor past the green navigational buoy near the reef pass and skirt tiny breakers that Riley mocks as "low on amps and voltage." Beer in hand, a tropic sea spread before his sunglass-clad eyes, Riley appears fully in his element, and accelerates us full-throttle into the blue water beyond the reef line. With low-prowed laminate hull, centered steering console, and canvas Bimini top, the Carolina Skiff projects a racy flair, which Riley accentuates with enthusiastic commentary. "High speed, low drag!" he shouts as the hull glances off wavelets like a skier through a mogul field, leaving a foam flurry in its wake. The more forceful impacts bounce me off my seat, prompting me to grab the railing for support. Steering westward, we draw a track parallel to the barrier reef. Soon, off our port bow, we catch a vista of the lush, sparsely-populated hills and valley characteristic of Pohnpei's northwest side.

Tapping me on the shoulder, Riley offers me a beer. "Enjoying the boat ride?" he asks, projecting his voice over the engine din.

"Absolutely!" I say. "This is fun!"

"In that case you probably won't mind if I tally your share of the costs."

"My share of the costs?"

"A boat ride can be expensive," he explains. "There's the cost of fuel, the cost of engine wear, the cost of beer. . ."

"I don't have to drink beer," I interject, hoping to limit my liability.

"You'll change your tune after a few hours of sun and salt."

"I didn't bring much cash," I stammer.

"Well, I'm not running a charity. Think of this as a recon operation that benefits you as much as me. With that in mind, I can extend you a line of credit." Holding up a notebook, he shows me a list of expenses already itemized.

"Mixed nuts?" I query, reviewing the list. "I haven't eaten any mixed nuts."

"Not yet. But you probably will."

Idling the engine, Riley steps back to the stern. From a box of fishing gear, he grabs a blue sardine-shaped lure and hooks it to a trolling line. He tosses the lure off the stern, reclaims his place at the helm, and motors us forward until about fifty yards of line spool into the water. He then locks the reel, and we continue our westward track at a leisurely pace. Meanwhile, shafts of sunlight prod the depths around us, flashing and dissipating, auroras in an aquatic atmosphere. I peer into the water, intrigued by the hypnotic display.

After several minutes, a gap appears in the line of turquoise and brown indicative of barrier reef some one hundred

147

yards shoreward. We angle toward the gap, motoring between two red mooring buoys which provide a lonely token of civilization in an otherwise empty sea. Off our port railing, the reef line curves into the lagoon, gradually at first and then abruptly like a horseshoe. The lagoon, mottled by a patchwork of submerged coral plateaus, broadly extends toward mangroves and mountains. Mindful of the reef, we putter toward a shallow area where craggy corals, rising to within fifteen feet of the lagoon surface, offer suitable grip for an anchor. Stepping to the bow, Riley sets the anchor and tests its fastness. He then turns off the engine, inducing a silence interspersed only by the soft whisper of breeze and the light smack of ripples lapping the skiff's underside. With a flourish of an emcee introducing a special attraction, he waves his arm toward the seascape.

"Palikir Pass," he presents. "One of the last secrets of the surf world."

Eddies of current swing the boat to and fro upon the tether of its anchor line. Wary of the dark clouds that mottle the eastern horizon, Riley suggests we embark on our snorkeling expedition before the weather turns. Grabbing a dive mask and a plastic disposable camera designed for underwater pictures, he enters the water, advising me to stay aware of the currents. "Don't stray too far from the reef," he warns, as I don a pair of swim-fins.

Peering underwater through my mask, I immerse myself in an aquatic wonderland where beams of refracted sunlight shimmer amid fish and coral crags. Striations of color, like sediments in a desert cliff, give a painted beauty to certain coral formations. Walls of vibrant yellow, roofed by brown plateaus, rise from purple foundations. Snorkeling past one such formation, I witness a chunk of yellow break off and swim away; a moment of surprise passes as I observe the chunk—really a fish seeking camouflage—stare back at me with bulbous eyes. I continue, guided by the trail of bubbles left by Riley's fins. Meanwhile, a slight current carries me toward an area of dark blue that marks the deep waters of the reef pass. Curious about what lies over the edge of the drop-off, I allow the current to take me. The reef slopes gradually away, and then plunges toward regions of dim illumination. There, perhaps one hundred feet below me, hazy finned forms—equipped, I imagine, with sharp teeth and hostile intent—glide about, shadows in the gloom. The sight quells my enthusiasm for further exploration of the abyss. Returning to the safety of the shallows, I catch up to Riley. Camera at the ready, he stalks a regal angelfish that flits among the coral heads and dazzles us with its Technicolor scales. Following the fish, we continue out another fifty yards. Along the seaward margins of the reef, small breakers crumble, their soft whispers a harmony to the sound of breath in my snorkel. Here, Palikir hints at its potential to create good surfing waves. From a line facing generally north-west, the reef makes a westward bend, creating a corner to focus the energy of incoming swells. Other than an anomalous bulge, formed by an outcrop of yellow coral, the reef's seaward edge tapers toward the reef pass as if drawn by a compass. Removing the snorkel from his mouth, Riley motions for me to surface.

"See that mountain summit?" he asks, pointing across the lagoon to the island skyline. "You can use it as a landmark to maintain position here. When you see it line up behind that smaller hill, you're in the main take-off spot."

"Really? What about that coral outcrop? Doesn't it make the wave section off?" I ask.

"Some waves swing wide of it, and can serve up a juicy inside bowl," he says. "However, the main peak forms here, along the twenty-yard section just below us." His eyes grow intense. "From here, you drop in, set your line, and . . .commit."

"Commit?"

"Commit to the flawless, pitching barrel that forms as the wave hits that outcrop; commit to the wall that makes your gaze a surfer's version of the thousand-yard stare."

I glance back along the line of reef toward the pass, my mind's eye conjuring an image of a fantasy wave that balances intensity and perfection. The image dissipates amid the reality of the current conditions, and recalling the conversation from the Rumours bar, I indeed see how a surf traveler could come to Pohnpei, look over the peaceful water, and leave without knowing the island's potential.

The sight of a frigate bird, landing upon the boat and pecking at something on the deck, dispels my musings. Agitated by the prospect of bird droppings on his boat and, worse, upon the canvas Bimini, Riley tells me to scare the bird away while he completes the camera roll.

A few minutes' steady kicking returns me to the boat. As I climb aboard, the bird wings aloft, dangling a red fishing lure from its beak. Deciding that I mean to permanently interrupt its cargo inspection, it departs for other ventures. Camera roll complete, Riley returns to the boat, removes his snorkeling gear, and tugs at the trolling line. Finding no resistance indicative of a hooked fish, he suggests that we try fishing the open waters beyond the reef. He starts the engine and idles the boat forward to put some slack in the anchor chain. He then steps to the bow, tugs on the chain, and mutters an expletive when the anchor refuses to budge from its coral perch. Frustrated, Riley asks me to "earn my beer" and dive down to manually free the anchor.

"I'll keep the boat in position over the reef, while you work the anchor free. It's probably just wedged into a chink in the coral," he says.

I don my mask and jump overboard. Drawing on a lungful of air, I swim down to where the miscreant metal glints silver against the coral brown. The effort proves more challenging than anticipated, for the current drags me off my bearing. Eventually, I reach the plateau, but my lungs, screaming for fresh oxygen, allow only a cursory attempt to pull the anchor free. I kick to the surface to re-group.

"Good initiative, bad judgement," Riley says, shaking his head.

"I didn't anticipate the current," I complain.

"Do I have to break it down Barney-style? Just use the anchor chain like a rope ladder and haul yourself down."

Filling my lungs once again, I follow the advice, reaching one hand below the other along the chain. This time I conserve my strength; grasping the anchor, I pull it free from the coral. Unfortunately, as I kick back to the surface, the devious device slips from my hand, only to lodge deeper than before.

"Aw hell," Riley vents, miffed by my empty-handed return to the surface. "You really do demonstrate significant FTA—failure to adapt. Get back on the boat."

Riley puts on a dive mask and jumps into the water. About thirty seconds later, he surfaces, anchor tucked in the crook of his arm. Treading water by the bow, he tells me to haul in the chain. He then pushes the anchor over the bow, and I stow it while he climbs aboard. Removing his mask, he flashes a look of displeasure.

"I need to know you count as a good piece of gear," he says. "I want only good gear in this outfit—that's mission critical. Understand? Now, the sooner you stop smoking and joking, the better. And you can forget about drinking any more of my beer." Admonition complete, he puts on his sunglasses and motors us through the lagoon toward the harbor.

Riley's capricious temperament, oscillating between the persona of a drill sergeant and a drinking buddy, makes me hesitant to pursue further conversation. I find an inconspicuous seat next to the snorkeling gear in the stern of the boat. The

151

thought of Riley as an abusive Captain Bligh, whip in one hand and Miller Lite in the other, lends a hint of comedy to the suddenly awkward atmosphere, but I stifle my laugh, and vent my nervous energy by tugging now and again on the trolling line. By the time we reach the shipping channel near Main Pass, the trolling line seems unusually taut, dragging a weight beyond that of the lure. I draw the matter to Riley's attention, whereupon he cuts the throttle and ventures a curious tug of his own.

Reeling in the line, Riley gradually works the mystery catch closer, and finally allows a triumphant grin to spread across his face as he pulls from the depths a beautiful deep-water snapper, red scales flashing iridescent in the sunlight. "Usually these fish stay outside the reef," Riley says. "It's a surprise catching one near the lagoon."

No sooner does Riley place the catch into the ice chest than the afternoon reveals another surprise. Like a rock star appearing un-announced upon the stage of a local bar, a set of long-period swells rise from the seaward depths of the reef pass. The first wave spins along the contour of the reef, forming a head-high barrel that, like a liquid eye, stares back at us as if to verify our interest. Two other waves repeat the performance. Dumbfounded, we watch in silence as the set dissipates in foam. The waves vanish as suddenly as they came, leaving us to ponder their significance.

"I'll be damned," Riley says, eyeing the once-again placid sea. "First a deep- water snapper, and then Main Pass comes to life. Hopefully we didn't just see a freak set, but rather a preview of things to come. The last forecast I checked held little promise, but that was several days ago. Probably I should have checked again this morning. Surf around here can come up fast."

The freak set kindles a sense of shared anticipation. When a frisky rainbow awakens from its cumulus bed, stretches a leg along the basalt face of Sokeh's Rock, and tickles the lagoon

152

Main Pass comes to life, November 1999. With a more northerly exposure and a deep water drop off, the reef here picked up the brunt of the swell, often producing surf at least twice as big as Palikir. The spot held serious size, and on big days, waves wrapped nearly 180 degrees around the horseshoe contour of the reef. Unfortunately (or fortunately, depending on one's perspective), getting it big and clean didn't happen very often, since the trade winds frequently blew a ragged chop into the line-up.

with its colorful toes, we see it as an omen of good things to come. "Tomorrow we'll bring surfboards instead of snorkels," Riley exults.

Drinking buddy once again, he offers me a beer, and whistles a cheerful tune while motoring us across the lagoon toward the causeway launch area.

The next morning, fortified with cash for my share of expenses, I arrive at Riley's doorstep. Anticipating another bout of fangs and fur, I relax when I see Stink Bomb and Fitty Cal far across the lawn, investigating a bearded countenance I soon recognize.

"Henrik!" I holler. "What are you up to?"

"I heard from the staff at the NOAA station there might be some swell coming in. So, I thought I'd look for a ride to the reef."

"There wasn't much yesterday, although we did see a freak set at Main Pass. We were hoping today might be better."

"It is better," Riley says, carrying an ice chest out to the boat. "I checked the buoy readings. The swell has filled in. Now saddle up, we're going Condition One."

After launching from the causeway ramp, we motor into a canopy of pastel blue from which cotton puff clouds hang in patches extending to the far horizon. For Riley, Henrik and me, projecting our gaze across the lagoon, the tropical sky matters less than the tropical sea, its surface lined with swells that march toward the barrier reef. Unlike the sporadic whitewater bursts of the day prior, today's swell paints an insistent swath of foam along the entire reef line. Meanwhile, the Carolina Skiff motors forth with an insistency of its own, reflecting the demeanor of its owner. Face expressionless behind dark shades, Riley commands an air of seriousness. When we buzz into the shipping channel and gain a clear glimpse of the surf, I understand why.

"Now there's some pucker factor for you," Riley says, as

an avalanche of whitewater tumbles in slow motion from the summit of a heaving roller. Main Pass resembles a budding big-wave spot, more appropriate for a heavy-water board than for my 6'10". I feel a tinge of relief when Riley points the prow westward and the skiff cuts a wake in the direction of Palikir. This time we navigate the lagoon side of the reef, allowing a frontal view of the breaking surf. Further west, the waves diminish, but what they lose in size they gain in form, their crests groomed by a breeze angling increasingly offshore. Henrik, peering through binoculars, eventually begins to whistle and grin. He hands the binoculars to me, and I too glimpse a tantalizing sight: the liquid corduroy of swell lines tapering perfectly along the bend of Palikir Pass. The sight turns the remaining minutes of our journey into a battle with impatience, made worse by shallow reef mesas that periodically force a reduction of speed. Finally, we pass the last of the hazards, and motor at a steady clip until the lagoon around us turns a dark blue and we enter the depths of Palikir Pass. Henrik and I stare in amazement at the surf, and when Henrik pulls out a video camera, Riley elects to anchor just inside the pass, to grant the camera a wide perspective of the line-up. For a few minutes, we stare mesmerized at waves that, painted in shades of tropic blue, repeatedly blow puffs of mist from their precision-crafted tubes. A dozen such waves work their magic before any of us stir.

"I reckon we could travel all over the Pacific and not find a better wave," Henrik says. "This is what surfers dream about — and we're here to live it!"

As if to help Henrik prove the point, one of the finest waves yet, aspiring to video fame, displays before Henrik's lens a fabulous turquoise tube that spins down the entire length of reef.

"Come on, Boys!" Henrik chortles, nearly dropping his camera. "Is this a spectator sport?"

"Not for long," Riley replies, transferring his attention

Palikir Pass, November 1999. Amid sunshine, gentle trades, and tropical hues, the physics of waves science yield to the ineffable aesthetic of the sublime.

from the surf to a bottle of sunblock. Henrik and I follow suit, and soon the boat deck changes from grandstand to staging area as we apply sunscreen, wax boards, and check leashes. Meanwhile, Riley advises us to keep an eye out for the dropping tide. "Less water means the inside section will dredge harder off the reef," he warns.

Preparations complete, we jump overboard and stroke our way to the surf.

Riley plucks the first flower from the wave garden. Enticed by a bloom of liquid morning glory, he angles into the pit, stands, and digs his heels into a backside bottom turn that slingshots him toward the inside section. While small ripples scallop the wave face, he passes by in a blur of speed, but not before blessing Henrik and I with a baptism of spray from a carving turn off the top.

Demonstrating a savvy wave sense—honed, perhaps, by his many months' experience feasting on a smorgasbord of Pacific island surf—Henrik positions himself in the takeoff zone just in time to stroke into a surging overhead wall. Angle-dropping down the face, he stalls briefly, allowing the wave's thin silver lip to curl first over his wake, then the tail of his board, and finally his shoulder and head. Emerging from the curtain, Henrik glides to the wave's still-sloping shoulder, and carves a cutback that exposes the bottom of his board down to the stringer. Bouncing off the foam ball of whitewater, he completes the maneuver and pumps for the inside section, which shoots him into the shallows. "That's what I'm talkin' about!" he cheers, completing his ride. I gesture a thumbs-up and scramble for the takeoff spot, eager for a taste of what Riley and Henrik just sampled.

A lull allows me to catch my breath before a bulge forms to seaward and lopes toward me. In contrast to the peeling wall Henrik caught, this wave concentrates its energy into a peak, its summit shimmering with a confluence of ripples. Paddling into

157

it, I descend a moving liquid ramp, mottled red and brown with the reflection of the reef. Speed bleeds from my rails as I lean into a bottom turn and zoom toward a wedging shoulder, where Henrik, voicing the universal exclamation of surf camaraderie, offers a "woot!" as I shoot by. Anticipating the dredge of the shallows, I traverse the trough, the wave a swirling sequence of reflections: coral heads, cotton puff clouds, island mountains draped in green. Locked in to the vortex, I adjust my stance for stability, as with a profusion of foam and spray the wave gives its spirit back to the sea.

And so we surf, trading sips from the chalice of Neptune, exulting in the articulations of pleasure to which surfers devolve when amped on adrenaline. Hours pass, but we forget fatigue, losing ourselves in a timeless realm where each wave offers a slice of the sublime. To the inside section, the dropping tide brings waves like crystal confections, bursting with a merengue of cotton-puff foam spun from the reflections of cotton puff clouds. In the take-off zone, blue peaks rise refulgent, crowned with silver plumes of mist. Like participants in a regal ceremony, they curl with precision, each one following its predecessor in an exquisite choreography where not a drop of water slips out of place.

Eventually, as the tide drops further, Riley, his wave selection modulated by an intuitive understanding of the swell, informs us that he "senses movement along the perimeter." Accordingly, he embarks on a "scouting mission" to the outside corner. Loath to leave the excitement of the main peak for the uncertainty of the frontier, Henrik and I stay behind, a decision that soon brings jealous regret. Rewarding Riley's intrepid intuition, the surf gods conjure from the sea a voluptuous vision that we recognize as the wave of the day. A rarified amalgam of liquid and light, it cavorts along the reef rim, tossing its lip like an exotic dancer tossing a veil. To the envy of his onlookers, Riley drops in, his board hung like a gleaming totem on the wall of an aquatic temple, divining the will of the wave. Accelerating from behind the peak, he backdoors his way into a flawless barrel, where, casually crouched, he returns our gazes, his eyes glazed with the magical mist of the tube. Emerging, he races a peeling wall all the way to the boat, his board a white blur visible through the back of the wave.

Eager to conclude my session with similar glory, I impatiently paddle to the outside corner, only to foolishly chase a low-tide phantom: a shifting shadow that turns to tenebrous trough. Too late, I prone away from the suck-out. The lip, brushing my back, knocks me off balance and facilitates an ignominious introduction between my rear end and the reef. I bounce along the coral shelf, the bubbly laughter of the wave's aftermath a sardonic rebuke for my ambition. Surfacing, I sprawl on my board, my muscles burning with forgotten fatigue. A lazy paddle brings me to the boat, where I find Riley toweling off in the shade of the Bimini.

"Care for a beer?" he asks.

"Sounds nice," I say, feeling the sting of a coral scrape spread along my thigh.

"Cash or credit?" Riley chuckles. "Between yesterday and today, you probably owe me about 25 bucks."

Thinking the sum a bargain for the priceless experience surfing Palikir Pass, I decide to splurge. "Just put it on my account," I say. "And add a can of mixed nuts."

Beers in hand, we while away several minutes in quiet contemplation, watching waves that, star performers in a dance of aquatic exuberance, mix power and elegance as the spin across the stage of Palikir Pass.

"It's a world class wave," I observe.

"Pretty darn good," Riley says.

Up the reef, a silhouette streaks across a sparkling wall, and we hear Henrik's chortled agreement come upon the breeze: "Yeah! That's what I'm talking about!"

Palikir Pass: Low tide and Northeast swell combine for an afternoon of mid-winter perfection. A deep-water reef pass has a defamiliarizing effect on those used to the psychological reassurance of a shoreline. Water moves in volumes unmitigated by benthic boundaries; the hypnotic sigh of the trade wind beguiles the mind; and the empty horizon constantly amplifies one's sense of isolation. Then a vision like this appears, and the strangeness of the setting accentuates the magical symmetry.

*   *   *

Excerpt from a Diary, November 1999:

Wandering the meadow above Fern Cove, I find a trail that leads into the hills. My explorer's spirit piqued, I crunch through shadows and shattered sunlight as the trail narrows to a footpath roofed by groping branches. A steamy ascent brings me to a ridgeline, beyond which the path descends into a ravine where the sound of plunging water resonates through the trees. As I proceed toward the sound, mist anoints my forehead, dissipating the heat with cool tingles. I thread my way through a stand of hardwoods and come to an abrupt ledge. Beneath me, set in a basin of basalt made glossy by the slow seep of moisture from the soil above, a forest pool shimmers, its waters set in motion by a waterfall about twenty feet high. Behind the cascade, a grotto, home to a colony of mosses and ferns, resembles a shrine draped by translucent silver beads.

The grotto beckons, and I descend to the pool, gingerly finding footholds on the wet rock. Reaching the water, I wade along the perimeter, and, shielding my eyes against the waterfall spray, squeeze into the grotto through the narrow gap between the waterfall and the rock face. Protruding from the roof of the grotto, a finger of rock splits the cascade, like a partition in a window curtain. Looking out from the grotto, I peer into a hidden world, sealed by a circle of sky that seems stamped from a cookie cutter and placed directly on the basalt basin's rocky rim. Through that sky clouds occasionally pass, white bouffant billows that I imagine as creatures of unknown essence and mysterious origin. Curtained by the cascade, I wonder what it would be like to reside in such a world, beneath that cookie-cut circle of sky. What gods would one invent? What myths would shape the narrative of existence? Then, examining the grotto, I find an answer, proffered via the enigmatic graffiti of a prior visitor whose sage wisdom, scratched upon an un-mossed stone, offers a simple philosophy: "pray for porn."

The grotto pool and waterfall, one of many in a land where mountain rainfall approaches 400 inches annually.

Chapter 8: Soursop, and other Enchantments

Synthesizer music, loud enough to rattle my apartment walls, startles me awake, each beat assaulting my ears with an insistent thud. As my initial shock fades, I soon recognize the song as one of the 1980's more annoying malconceptions.

You spin me right round baby round round, blare the lyrics. *Like a record baby round round, round round.*

The displeasure of hearing the song so loudly resurrected—at 7:00 a.m. on a Saturday, for that matter—soon gives way to intrigue. Could all this chaos really emanate from the apartment of Jasper, my respectable neighbor and colleague? Curious if Jasper's scholarly demeanor and poetic sensibility mask the persona of a budding party animal, I decide to investigate.

You spin me right round baby round round.

"Jasper? You OK?" I holler, voice projected through the rattling wallboard that separates our dwellings. The music drowns out my inquiries. Heading outside to knock on his door, I find an unfamiliar scene. In place of my view of water and mountains, I find laundry—sheets, towels, shirts, and underwear—hung upon a clothesline. In place of birds pecking papaya, I find a pair of half-naked kids chasing each other among the hanging garments.

"Uh. . .Jasper?" I stammer, just before chips, the Sheldon's dog, charges me from across the lawn and muddies my shoulders with his forepaws. Excited by the ruckus, Chips musters enough momentum to knock me backwards on the grass, perfume my face with dog-breath, and douse my shirt with slobber. No doubt wanting me to throw something for him to fetch, he adds a few barks to the general cacophony.

Like a record baby round round.

Prone on the grass and thoroughly bewildered, I look up to see a shapely island lass step out Jasper's door and peer at my embarrassment. The woman covers her mouth with her hand, giggles shyly, and then points toward me. As I stagger to my feet, the music quiets, and Jasper emerges in the doorway.

"Er. . .Jacques," Jasper announces. "I'd. . .uh. . .like you to meet my wife, Rosaleen." Uncomfortable with the introductions,

Rosaleen looks at her toes and fingers a bracelet. "She and her kids are taking up residence with me here at Fern Cove."

The news, like a radio signal wrapped in static, sounds in my ears but registers reluctantly in my brain. Meanwhile, Rosaleen's kids, their cherubic faces a spite to my growing displeasure, climb onto the hood of my car and battle to see who can push the other off first.

"Uh. . .congratulations!" I voice mechanically, nonplussed by the morning's mayhem.

Returning inside, I take a few moments to recover my wits and replace my dog-muddied shirt and shorts with some more presentable garments. However, my rummaging finds nothing suitable; my own laundry festers in a sorry state of neglect. Seeing Rosaleen's clothesline as a symbol of my own forsaken chores, I decide to load my laundry into my car and seek the convenience of a coin-operated laundromat in town. As I porter my laundry bag across the lawn, the kids discover that jumping simultaneously on my car's front bumper makes the shock absorbers compress and spring back. The phenomenon produces a newfound game for them and a newfound annoyance for me. Finally, my exasperation peaks when Rosaleen, rather than scolding her kids for their wonton assault on my property, instead giggles with enjoyment at their antics.

"Get off my car!" I growl.

My surly tone makes the kids scurry for the protection of their mother. Clinging to her skirt, one of them starts to cry. Rosaleen scowls at me as though my outburst represents a transgression of island etiquette. A look of mutual embarrassment passes between Jasper and me, just before a flurry of raindrops adds a new drama. Torn between the emotional need to console her children and the practical need to rescue the drying garments from the rain, Rosaleen shrieks a few words in Pohnpeian. As she and Jasper undo clothespins, I drive off, smug in my decision to use the laundromat, where electric dryers confer immunity to the vagaries of weather.

As I cross the bridge toward Kolonia, my annoyance with the morning gives way to meditative reflection. Perhaps, I muse, the morning's foibles represent a karmic kick-in-the-pants, retribution for the hedonistic bent I allowed my life to take since the advent of surf season. For weeks, dreaming increasingly of Palikir's perfect waves, I placed my teaching on auto-pilot, while my telephone functioned as a hotline to Riley Schroff, who conducted daily surf reconnaissance with the seriousness of a military planner and kept me updated on when to expect the best combination of tide, wind, and swell. Now, I see the bill for my surf obsession itemized in a few significant ways. In addition to my laundry, a box of un-graded papers, forgotten on the floorboard below the passenger seat, awaits my attention, while a ragged scruffiness on my chin belies my neglected personal hygiene.

Against these self-recriminations, the rain presents a delightful deluge. Indifferent to guilt or grievance, it taps a patter-dance rhythm through the streets, twirls a skirt of diamond drops over rooftops and ravines, and leaps toward the ridge, coating the crags with a silver sheen. In its wake the air seems alive, infused with ethereal invitations.

Typical of Kolonia's haphazard urban planning, the laundromat occupies a grassy lot full of wandering chickens that add a barnyard clamor to the morning. Surprisingly, despite the early hour, I find many of the laundromat's machines already humming, as a tall blond woman in a pinafore dress flits about, intently placing tokens into coin slots. Sitting in a corner, a silver-bearded man—momentarily distracted from his book-reading by my entrance—glances toward me, his stern demeanor projected by a posture so unbent as to make one think that the integrity of his character depended on the straightness of his spine.

"Good morning, son!" he says with a deep-chested bellow. Alerted to my presence, the woman gives me an angelic smile.

"Good morning," I reply. "I didn't expect to find anyone here so early."

"Never too early for the Lord's work," the man says, placing the book, which I now recognize as a Bible, on his lap. "Nor too early for laundry. 'Wash yourselves, make yourselves clean, and take your evil deeds from my sight'—Isiah 1:16," he quotes, drawing the words from some wellspring of memory that requires him to momentarily close his eyes. "Of course, a clean garment may cloak a sinful heart—in which case, one must seek the purification of prayer."

"Amen" the woman intones. She deposits a final token, and the sound of whirring washers reminds me to locate a machine of my own.

"Where you from, son?" the man asks.

"California," I reply. Hoping for an interaction of a more amiable variety than what transpired at Fern Cove, I assume a friendly demeanor and introduce myself. I mention the word "teacher," and the man nods solemnly.

Standing, he shakes my hand. "Pleased to meet you, Jacques. I'm Holton Sloan, and this devout woman is my wife, Debbie. We too consider ourselves teachers, though perhaps of a different sort. People look to us not for grades, but for understanding of the Christian faith. Tell me, Jacques—have you found the peace that comes from devotion to the Lord?"

I consider the question with an angst augmented by memories of my recent foray into organized religion. Less than a year earlier, in preparation for a church wedding, my ex-fiancée and I undertook the "marriage inventory" process recommended by her family's Catholic diocese. Under the pallid proctoring of Father Ron, a callous official determined to portray me as an

169

infidel unworthy of the salvageable churchgoer dormant in my bride-to-be, the inventory process drove a wedge of Catholic guilt into a once-thriving intimacy. The resulting conflict, a contributing factor in the eventual wedding cancellation, left me with an abiding resentment of the Church. If Jesus saves, I thought, then let him save me from his followers.

Fortunately, before I express this sentiment to Holton, his wife intervenes. "Now Holton, go easy," Debbie says, giving her husband a wink that softens her tone of admonishment. "The poor fellow just wants to do his laundry, not listen to a sermon." With motherly concern, she leads me to a vacant washing machine, donates a cupful of soap to my cause, and informs me that when my clothes need drying, she has sheets of fabric softener to spare.

I thank Debbie for her generosity and load my laundry into the machine. Meanwhile, Holton returns to his Bible. From the way he mumbles certain passages aloud and casts sideways glances my direction, I can sense him chafing against his wife's admonition. Accordingly, thinking some industrious grading might shield me from any Bible discussion, I start the wash, head to my car, and return with a stack of student papers. I manage to mark a few before I hear the approach of footsteps and see Debbie admire my efforts.

"My, look at you hard at work!" she commends. "Before the Church sent us out as missionaries, I taught high school, so I know about grading a stack of papers. Your wife and kids must find inspiration in your devotion to students."

Embarrassed by the truth, I look in Debbie's eyes and imagine forgiveness and compassion. "Maybe if I had a wife and kids, I'd stay more focused," I reply. I explain how my current diligence represents an attempt to catch up on several weeks' worth of chores which my bachelor distractions left neglected.

Debbie gives me an expression of surprised concern.

"You live without family on this island?" she ponders. "That's sad to hear, especially this time of year. Why, back home, folks just celebrated Thanksgiving! If you have no one to celebrate with, you can join our family for a belated feast this evening at Sei restaurant." Raising her voice above the machine din, she solicits her husband's agreement to the invitation.

"Sure," Holton hollers back, fingering his Bible. "Jacques may find dining among Christians provides all the family he needs."

Thanksgiving? Had I really forgotten the holiday? Briefly, my mind flashes an image of mainland friends and family, enjoying a bounty of fresh foods while, alone in Micronesia, I poke a fork into a meagre meal conveyed from a can. Confronted with the prospect of my lonely repast, I consider Debbie's invitation. Then, I remember the word "missionaries." Picturing myself dining alongside several Bible-quoting proselytizers, I rescind my enthusiasm.

"Uh. . .well. . ." I stammer, trying to think of a diplomatic way to refuse. "I'd really like to join you, but. . ." My excuse stalls on my lips, as into the laundromat struts a young brunette. Like Salome tossing a veil, the girl removes her raincoat, revealing bare shoulders caressed by the fabric of a spaghetti-strap blouse. Focusing her emerald eyes on Debbie, the girl crinkles the tip of her nose.

"Mom!" she says. "This place smells like a detergent factory! Are you using too much soap again?"

"Relax, Jessica," Debbie says calmly. "A little soap never hurt anybody. Now, Jacques here was about to say whether he'd like to join us for Thanksgiving dinner."

Sparkling her eyes on me, the girl shines with enticing energy. "Oh, the Sei buffet is just the best!" she proclaims.

"What time should I meet you?" I ask.

"Six o'clock," Debbie says.

"I'll be there."

That evening, showered and groomed, I find the missionaries in the reception area of Sei Restaurant. Twilight purples, diffusing through the restaurant's broad bay windows, burnish a floor of hardwood planks and reflect upon the face of the Japanese proprietor, who bows his head in greeting. While the proprietor and a demure hostess arrange tables for our party of Thanksgiving celebrants, we eye the buffet and its display of sumptuous morsels: tuna sashimi, vibrantly pink, arranged like a spiral of dominoes on a platter; steamed eggplant, coated in black bean sauce, gleaming with a savory glow; vegetable fried rice, piled in a mound inhabited by peas and carrots. These and other items invite me to discard my expectation that Thanksgiving means cranberries and stuffed turkey. The discovery that ten dollars buys admission to this all-you-can-eat wonderland enhances my salivation. When I grow restless from eyeing the food, I contemplate the view. Extending into the twilight behind the windows, a lush valley, bordered by cloud-shrouded peaks, spreads a panorama of primal possibility, and I picture frolicking through the forest with Jessica. Meanwhile, my ears fill with the hungry banter of my fellow diners—Holton's family, a few other missionaries, plus a handful of island youths whose enthusiasm for feasting remains undiminished by their ignorance of the American holiday which occasioned the celebration.

While the proprietor prepares our tables, we follow Holton's lead to the buffet and line up to load our plates. Enticed by the food-fest, I pile my plate with morsels. Jessica, selecting dainty portions, reminds me of my manners. Not wanting to appear greedy, I return an egg roll to the warming tray, but Holton puts a reassuring hand on my arm. "Eat, drink, and be joyful," he advises, piling his plate with goodies. "Ecclesiastes 8:15."

Holton takes his seat, waits for the remaining celebrants to do the same, and says a quick word of grace which, perhaps out of eagerness to start his meal, he leaves uncharacteristically bereft of Bible quotes. Then, turning attention to his plate, he surprises me by coating his sashimi with enough wasabi mustard to cauterize his taste buds.

"Thought I was just a Bible-banging old man, didn't you?" Holton says, enjoying the shocked expression I give him after he consumes several wasabi-saturated tuna slices. "I won the pepper competition at the Fulton County fair three years in a row. No one could chew the habanero peppers longer than I."

"That's quite a talent," I remark.

"With the help of Jesus, a person can do just about anything," Holton tells me, his voice projecting down the table. "Whenever you face a challenge, think of Jesus upon the cross, and know your own sufferings pale in comparison."

Debbie and several other missionaries respond with nods of approval, and the atmosphere grows thick with theopathy. "So Jessica," I say, eager to turn the conversation away from religion, "what special talents do you have?"

"Nothing really," she says, taking a napkin to dab a white kernel of rice from her lip. "At least, nothing that would earn me a prize at the county fair."

"Jess is just being modest," Debbie says, placing an affectionate hand on her daughter's shoulder. "God gave her a fantastic singing voice. I know it was God gave it to her, since neither Holton nor I sing any better than crows."

"Wow," I say. "I hope I get a chance to hear you sing, Jessica."

"That's easy enough," Holton says, halting his fork and fixing me in an intent gaze. "Just come to church with us tomorrow."

The valley behind Sei restaurant. Good food and views like this made the ten-dollar buffet price a bargain.

I wince, pierced by the horns of a dilemma. Any excuse to avoid church will render my words to Jessica no better than a flirtation. Jessica, sensing as much, smirks as I struggle for a response. Gritting my teeth, I realize my pursuit of Jessica might require a greater investment than dinner. "I look forward to it," I lie, taking a sip of iced tea to moisten my suddenly dry mouth.

"Perhaps you'll discover something you didn't expect," Jessica says, giving me a strangely mischievous smile.

"What do you mean?" I prod.

"We often get so focused on our personal wants that we ignore the true beauty around us. For example, consider this buffet."

"The buffet?"

"You've devoted so much of your plate to sashimi and fried rice that you overlooked the best thing on the menu."

"What's that?" I ask, wondering if she includes herself in the list of overlooked things.

Jessica silently stands, heads to the buffet table, and returns with a small plate containing wedges of what looks like delicate albino pineapple.

"This," she says, her voice quietly reverent, "is soursop." Placing a white wedge in her mouth, she chews slowly, as though each movement of her jaw releases from the fruit fresh flavors that require time to appreciate. "Mmm. . ." she murmurs, pushing the plate toward me.

I take a sample, and marvel at the array of flavors that seduce my palate. As I chew, a hint of smooth cream coats my tongue. Sweetness, airy and ambrosial, activates taste buds I never knew I had.

"Isn't that just amazing!" Jessica exclaims, her lower lip shiny with juice. Leaning across the table, she pokes her fork into another soursop wedge and brings the fruit to her tongue. A light scent of perfume, wafting from her neck like fragrance from a

175

flower, tickles my nose.

"Amazing," I agree.   Perhaps intoxicated by the ambrosial fruit, the perfume, and more than anything, Jessica's sudden proximity, I blurt, "but not half as amazing as you."

Blushing, Jessica quickly sits back, glances at her father, and uses a napkin to wipe the shiny soursop juice from her lip. I half expect to hear a Puritan rebuke from Holton, but he pays no heed to my indiscretion and gorges on his meal.

"Perhaps you notice that little bit of God that shines in all of us," Jessica says demurely. "If you come to church tomorrow, you can see it all around you."

Accordingly, on the Sunday after Thanksgiving, I drive into Kolonia to attend church with the missionaries, my romantic designs augmented by a night spent re-playing the image of soursop juice trickling down Jessica's lips. A fresh sun paints the morning with exuberant radiance, which my romantic aspirations take as a good omen. Arriving at an old stone church, whose arched entryway and turreted bell tower reprise a European architecture, I park by a broad green lawn, and see Holton and Debbie unloading plastic cups, bags of chips, and soda from the trunk of a white sedan.   I amble their direction, scanning anxiously for Jessica.

"Jacques!" Holton greets me. "Through prayer and some assistance from the Lord, we've arranged some more favorable weather this morning. I find nothing quite so uplifting to my spirit as the gleam of sunshine through a church's stained-glass windows."

Debbie, concerned for the moment with matters practical rather than spiritual, asks me if I can carry a blue Coleman chest to the picnic tables behind the church. "It's too heavy for me, and with Holton having back trouble, I thought you could help."

"Planning a party?" I ask, eyeing the soda and chips. I hoist the ice chest into my arms. Cool and moist, it feels loaded with ice cubes and soda.

"More like a picnic," Debbie says. "After church, we often have an informal gathering to discuss our work and plans."

Sure that "informal gathering" translates to prayer and proselytizing, I feel my heart sink as I trudge forth upon my chore. Then I glimpse Jessica by the church entrance, her dress catching the sun like a burst of plumeria, and my lustful ambitions put a spark in my step—a spark soon smothered by the combination of heavy ice chest and tropical heat. By the time I reach the picnic tables, my brow drips a pernicious perspiration. Relinquishing my burden, I reach inside the ice chest for a soda, and a gleam catches my eye. On the ground beside the picnic table, in the company of a cigarette package, a paper bag, and a pink barrette—the detritus, no doubt, of some midnight tryst—a partially consumed bottle of Bacardi sparkles in the morning light. *Drink and be joyful*, I muse, regarding the rum as a blessing of "nerve tonic" to succor my stamina. *Ecclesiastes 8:15!* Whatever picnic proselytizing the missionaries intend, I'll endure it better with some rum-infused refreshment. Accordingly, I guzzle half the contents of a soda, refill the can with rum, and put the concoction aside for later enjoyment. As I apply the process to a second can, approaching voices interrupt my ad-hoc alchemy. Hastily, I hide the Bacardi and soda behind the ice chest.

"Sorry to be such a nuisance," Debbie says, placing a bag of fruit on the table. "Do you mind helping us with another load?"

"Uh. . .no problem," I stammer, moving the ice chest to better conceal my mischief.

"We'll just bring out the rest of the fruit," she says. "Then we best get inside, as the service is about to start." Following Debbie, I adjust the collar of my shirt, and assume my best demeanor.

Stepping inside the church, I find most of the

177

congregation already seated. Worried that the true believers might divine my charlatan ways, I seek an unobtrusive seat in a back pew. Meanwhile, light from a stained-glass window makes the church bloom with color, and illuminates the finery of island ladies, who wear dresses of blue or purple hemmed with frills of white lace. The men, dressed in immaculate white, look toward the pulpit, patiently waiting for the service to begin. Along a wall to the left of the pulpit stands a choir, Jessica radiant among them.

Over the next hour, following the lead of those around me, I stand, sit, mouth along to hymns, and try to impersonate a devoted churchgoer, all the while casting hopeful glances at Jessica. Demure among the choir, Jessica seems to have eyes only for the image of Jesus that adorns the wall behind the pulpit. As my glances go unrequited, I eventually content myself with listening to her voice, which, during hymns, comes to my ears as a siren song, more sonorous than the voices around me. The more I listen, the more alluring grows the voice, until I hear it in my ears even after the singing stops.

Thus enchanted, I step boldly into the sunlight of the after-service gathering, intending to declare my affections. Playing gentleman, I offer Jessica a soda, and then sit across from her, hoping to begin with some flirtatious small talk. Unmoved by my arrival, Jessica dotes on a little girl seated alongside her. Perhaps five years old, the little girl lolls her tongue and drools saliva on her chin as Jessica holds her.

"Hi sweetie! What's your name?" I croon, hoping that my efforts to endear myself to the child will, in turn, endear me to Jessica. Leaning closer to the girl, I see she must be in the throes of some stomach ailment, or so I infer from the way she clutches her tummy.

"She's sick," Jessica says. "Some idiot poured rum into this soda can and just left it out here. Can you believe that? Silverina was thirsty, so of course she drank it. Poor girl."

"Gosh, I'm sorry to hear that," I say, feeling genuine guilt and sympathy, but loath to admit my role in the matter.

"I tell you, there's some real sickos in this world!" Jessica says.

Devoted to Silverina's care and comfort, Jessica mostly ignores me, and even when I praise her singing she responds with barely a grunt. With my romantic aspirations thwarted, I lament ever finding the Bacardi bottle, lest the liquor prove my undoing. Still, transfixed by the angelic way in which Jessica soothes Silverina, I linger at the table, like a dog jealous for attention. And, like a dog that advertises its presence by yelping and whining, I recall the tale of my own last hangover, incurred during the dark days of my broken engagement with my ex-fiancée. In my quest for pathos I cast myself a bit too much as the victim but justify such hyperbole as a necessary means to an end.

"You poor thing," Jessica says.

"Well, I'm getting over it. . .time heals all wounds," I reply.

"Huh?" Jessica says, apparently hearing me for the first time. "No, I mean poor Silverina. I don't want her getting sick in front of all these people. I better find a way to get her home."

Eager to inveigle some alone-time with Jessica, I quickly volunteer my car for the trip. Jessica agrees, though with no great excitement, and goes to inform her father, who presides at a nearby table. Holton looks concernedly my direction and mouths some quiet words to his daughter.

"Don't worry, Dad," I hear Jessica say. "I have the ability to distinguish sin from sanctity in the human heart."

Holton approaches me and rests a hand on my shoulder. "Well Jacques, you're leaving us sooner than I hoped. Do you think you might join us in the future?"

"I'm tempted," I say, unable to pry my eyes from Jessica.

Holton grins. "In that case, be comforted in the

179

knowledge that God will not let you be tempted beyond your ability—Corinthians 10:13."

With Silverina in tow, Jessica and I walk across the lawn to my car. After arranging Silverina in the back seat, Jessica reclines in the passenger seat and, to my surprise, pulls a pack of cigarettes from her handbag. As I put the car in gear, Jessica lights up, rolls down the window, and lets the breeze fluff her hair.

"I'm sorry about my dad," she sighs. "He can get a little excessive with the Bible stuff."

"Really?" I say. "I hadn't noticed."

Jessica curls her mouth into a smirk. "Last night at dinner, the way you kept staring at me. . . I thought for sure he would start spouting fire and brimstone."

Still playing gentleman, I feign ignorance of the accusation. "You think I—"

"Don't pretend you weren't," she interrupts, though her indignation seems half-hearted. "The way you watched me eat that soursop, I thought you might lean across the table and lick the juice off my lips. I know about guys like you."

Wondering what she means by "guys like me," I drive toward Silverina's neighborhood in the jungly hinterland behind Kolonia. We ascend a fern-clad slope, and then enter a cool ravine where the asphalt beneath my car gives way to a dirt road barely worthy of the term. Wary of ruts and oil-pan denting rocks, I nudge us forward at a crawl.

"Truth be told, sometimes all the church stuff gets a little overwhelming," Jessica confides.

"Really?" I say, glad to have the topic shift away from my dinner behavior. "Everyone seems quite nice."

"Oh sure," she says. "But sometimes I need a break. Problem is, I don't have any friends out here. . . no real friends, anyway. Sure, my father says that I always have a friend in Jesus, but, well. . .a girl needs a little fun now and then." She says this with a tone that rekindles my romantic aspirations.

We come to a rubble of boulders that, apparently fallen from the hillside, forces me to swerve far into the bracken along the road shoulder. Letting the engine idle us forward, I lean out the driver's window and scan ahead to make sure no tire-piercing thorns await. Casually, Jessica places her hand on my leg.

"By the way, I didn't mind for you to kiss me," she says softly.

"Really?"

"Well, not at dinner, but maybe after, when no one was looking," Jessica says.

"I would never have guessed," I say.

"Maybe you should kiss me now," Jessica says. She taps her cigarette ash out the window and flashes me a coquettish glance. "You know you want to."

Distracted by Jessica's transformation from angelic beauty to sultry temptress, I jolt us into a pothole. In the back seat, Silverina squirms and moans. Turning to voice my apologies to the passengers, I see Jessica's eyes flush red and a tear descend her cheek.

"I bet you just think I'm a tramp," she whimpers.

"You're sweet and beautiful," I say, reaching a comforting arm toward her.

"I'm just so lonely. . .so bored and lonely on this island," Jessica explains. "I hardly have any friends here."

A pang of sorrow runs through me as Jessica's words conjure ghosts from my own half-forgotten mainland life.

"Maybe we can be friends," I offer, stopping the car to console my companion. "Next week, after church, I'll drive us up to the college and see if we can access some music equipment. Maybe I can accompany you on guitar. I know a few tunes."

Jessica wipes the tear from her cheek and surprises me with a laugh. Pushing away from my embrace, she opens the passenger door.

"Let's cut the crap, o.k.?" she says, making her exit from the car. "You don't want to be my friend any more than you want to attend church. You're just play-acting so you can make some moves on me." Gathering Silverina from the back, she sighs. "So, I decided to do a little play-acting of my own. You sleazebag. . .I see though your little game. We all know who poured that rum in the Coke can. I hope you feel rotten for making poor Silverina sick."

I mumble some words that sound like gibberish. Jessica, unsympathetic, continues her departure.

"While people like you delight in personal lusts, some of us seek the light of the Lord," Jessica concludes, leading Silverina on foot down the road. Sunshine, filigreed by its passage through a canopy of overhanging branches, spreads about them, coalesces on Jessica, and radiates from her dress. She pauses and turns around.

"Sleazebag!" she yells.

Peals of denunciation chime through the ravine.

*　　　*　　　*

Excerpt from a Diary, December 1999

Moisture inescapable: three days of rain render my abode a dank cave, dampening my clothes and bedsheets, swelling the wallboards, a making a mealy pulp of toilet paper, its 2-ply absorbency a magnet for the saturated air. Though I recall a time of feather-cloud skies, warmly lit by a thing called a sun, the memory seems unreal, like an extract from a dream, or a delusion conjured by an inmate of the rain prison to cope with confinement.

Inmate in a prison of rain — darkly poetic, the phrase could title a noir portrayal of the expat life on Pohnpei; thinking about it prods me to reflect upon the psychology of place. For Conrad, crafting his classic novella Heart of Darkness, *the defamiliarizing quality of the African jungle — at once exotic and fearsome — provided a suitable undertone to the disconcerting themes of the narrative. One wonders, did landscape serve merely as literary trope, a rhetorical wrapper in which to place a story, or more fundamentally, did landscape let loose the narrative, such that only African jungle could have made Conrad's tale so dark? Inevitably, the question prods me to examine the power of place upon my own experience. Perhaps I languish in the climate equivalent of delirium tremens: five months removed from California, I suffer from the withdrawal of its steady-state sunshine, and thus find a preternatural quality in a rain event the islanders consider routine. Until I acclimate, my anxious mind attributes to the weather an oppressive character: rain relentless, and moisture inescapable.*

Chapter 9: Rumbles in the Mist

Riley Schroff examines the case of beer suspiciously, believing European imports beyond the reach of my English teacher's salary. "Heineken?" He marvels. "You can't afford that!"

I offer the case in a spirit of holiday cheer, but nevertheless feel like a vassal bringing tribute to a lord. Riley, assessing the packaging and contents, plucks an iconic green bottle from the case, and removes the bottle cap. After a satisfying swig, he lets his doubt give way to enthusiasm.

"I'll be damned," he says.

"I figure we could use something special to ring in the New Year," I say, inviting myself to a sofa seat near the T.V. The number of Miller Lite cans populating the vicinity hint at celebratory preparations already underway.

"A case of beer and a spot on the sofa—that's your big plan for New Year's Eve?" Riley asks sarcastically.

"Hey, if you don't like it, I can take the beer someplace where it might find more appreciation. I know a few parties."

"Not so fast," Riley says, arranging his fridge to make room for the new inventory. "You owe me at least this much for all the times I've boated you to the reef." Bottles clink as Riley stows the beer. Between clinks, he suggests a party plan more to his liking. "Now, if you brought over a few of those cute co-eds from the college, I might get more excited."

"No co-eds," I say. "I'm still recuperating from my last ill-fated attempt at romance." I recount my Thanksgiving adventure, and my unrequited pursuit of the missionaries' daughter.

Returning to the sofa, Riley smirks and wags his finger unsympathetically. "Your love-quest was doomed to failure," he says. "The next time you court a girl, do yourself a favor and consult with me first. I could offer a few tips."

"Such as?" I prod.

"For one thing, any objective observer can detect the emotional baggage you carry around. How many more times do you intend to subject people to that melodramatic tale of how you broke up with your fiancée? Girls want a guy who projects confidence, not a broken heart."

Anticipating a barrage of criticism, I head to the fridge to grab a beer of my own. Recriminations pursue me into the kitchen.

"Your next mistake," Riley continues, with increasing vehemence, "was to pursue courtship under the delusional presumption that this girl wanted you to act like a gentleman. In my experience, women like men of action, not manners."

"Is that so?" I reply, swigging my way to the sofa. Courtesy of CNN, sporadic scenes from New Year's Eve celebrations in New Zealand and Australia flash upon the T.V.

"Absolutely."

"I see." The televised sounds of New Year's revelry seem faint and distant, afraid to intercede against the critique.

"Do you?" Riley says. "Perhaps you don't. Your inability to close the deal with this girl could have implications. Word gets around."

"What do you mean?" I ask.

"All my friends are successful people. They know me as a guy who can accomplish things—a man of action, so to speak. If word gets around that Riley Schroff hangs out with a guy who can't close the deal, well, that affects my reputation. I have a reputation to uphold."

"What do you want me to do?" I ask apologetically, feeling responsible for the increased agitation in the room.

"I want you to man up!" Riley says, his face flushing red. "I prefer to associate with successful people—folks who can help me rise through the ranks of achievement, not inhibit me with incompetence. Now, just answer plainly. Are you the type of associate I can count on?"

"I can try," I stammer.

"Fortunately, we don't have to wait long to put your efforts to the test," Riley grins. "The swell forecast shows a big swell coming. You should have plenty of opportunity to man up."

We beer-belch our way through the remainder of the evening and let CNN's images of New Year's revelry allow us vicarious participation in the global welcome of the new millennium. By the time we tire of televised replays that show fireworks bursting above Sydney's iconic Harbour Bridge, a delicate camaraderie, built upon inebriation and the prospect of surf, re-emerges. I wish Riley a happy New Year and depart. In reply, I receive warning not to pilfer any of the remaining Heinekens.

New Years' Day dawns gunmetal gray, the sky a pewter lid fastened upon the rim of the sea. Eager to greet the forecasted swell, we motor across the lagoon, our gazes probing the reef line. Suspended in the atmosphere, a sheet of mist obscures our view. As we draw near the shipping channel buoy, the engine strains against a roiling current. Riley idles the engine and peers seaward to assess the conditions.

We hear the surf before we see it. A low rumble, growing in volume, foreshadows a vision of doom. Thundering along the reef, an avalanche of whitewater roars past. Tiny droplets of foam, flung skyward by the chaos, hang suspended in the air like moisture from an oceanic sneeze. With a newfound respect for the swell, we motor with a slow deliberation towards Palikir, our eyes growing wider with each liquid supernova that flashes through the mist.

Arriving at Palikir, we thread the boat through a hostile seascape. Cross currents and confused ripples agitate the normally calm channel. We aim for the coral outcrop that serves as our preferred anchorage, but the flow of water, spilling over the reef and into the lagoon, makes steering difficult. Accordingly, Riley heads for the deeper water seaward, thinking to moor to the channel buoy. This plan presents a different difficulty; grabbing the buoy as it bobs upon the deep-water swells requires careful timing. Finally, Riley motors in close, waits as we crest a swell, and commands me to grab the loop of thick rope that sprouts from the buoy's top. As buoy and boat descend into the trough of an oncoming swell, I hang on, while Riley cuts the engine, dashes to the bow, and deftly lashes a mooring line to the buoy rope. Thus positioned, we gain a less mist-impeded view of the surf. What I see vanquishes any remaining confidence, nursed until now in a warm corner of my ego, that I can handle such conditions. A lurching, liquid monster, its boil-marred mouth capable of devouring a school bus, sends a shiver of fear down my spine.

"The swell is just too intense," I proclaim. "My board just wasn't designed for waves like this. I need a board with more paddle power." Under the circumstances, blaming my timidity on my equipment seems entirely reasonable, and has the bonus of preserving a bit of my dignity, or so I think.

To my surprise, and momentary relief, Riley agrees. "The swell has a lot of power—more than forecast. Our shortboards just aren't appropriate." A solemn expression on his face, he steps aft and pulls aside a tarp, revealing a pair of longer, thick-glassed boards. Possessing all the big-wave design features supposedly absent in my own equipment, the new boards deprive my excuse of legitimacy. "Good thing I opted to bring the semi-guns," Riley says, examining the boards' leash plugs. "I'll ride the 7'6" and you can ride the 7'5". I think you'll find it provides plenty of paddle power."

Deprived of my first excuse, I seek vainly for others: the prospect of a better tide, or the possibility that our kidneys need more time to fully process any trace alcohol left over from our Heineken-infused New Year's celebration. Unfortunately, I know full well that the cramps in my stomach arise not from a hangover, but from nerves, as my companion displays his resolve to paddle out. After applying sunblock to his face, he rubs a bar of wax over the deck of the 7'6". When he hands the wax to me, I cringe, like a condemned man being shackled by his executioner.

"See you out there," Riley says. With maniacal mirth, he jumps from the boat and begins his foray to the surf.

Salvaging a thread of determination from my tattered resolve, I wax the glossy deck of the 7'5" and try to calm the panic that flutters my heart when I ponder leaving the sanctuary of the boat. Finally, I evaluate my predicament in rational terms. Paddling out, I theorize, represents a completely different enterprise from riding waves; doing the former creates no obligation to do the latter. Accordingly, I devise a scheme: sit just close enough to the takeoff zone to look serious about riding waves, but remain safely enough seaward to avoid catching one. Deluded with my plan, I jump overboard, cradling the 7'5" like a life-preserver.

Prone on the semi-gun, paddling cautiously through the opaque sea, I gain a more visceral sense of the swell. Wild warbles disrupt the gray horizon, arch their backs like newly-wakened beasts, and charge me aggressively, hinting at the anger of the storm that spawned them. Near the reef, where mist rises like smoke from a battlefield, booms and crashes attest to the sea's violent disposition. As I approach the takeoff zone, where Riley sits in stoic disregard of the turmoil, the walled swells push ahead of them airy drafts that howl in my ears. Warily, I angle to what I perceive as the region of safety, sit upright, and realize that sometime between when I jumped off the boat and when I reached my current location, I entered the realm of idiocy.

"Can you feel it?" Riley hollers. "Can you feel the POWER?"

A half-hearted nod represents all the enthusiasm I can muster.

"Days like this are when you put it all on the line," Riley says. "Any clown can ride six-foot perfection and look good. It takes a real surfer to paddle out in macking swell and take a bomb

190

from the outside corner. Clown or surfer—what do you want to be?"

I gaze at the maelstrom of whitewater that marks the point where the incoming swells disembowel themselves on the far promontory of reef, and decide a clown suit fits me just fine. To my skeptical eyes, the waves look hardly rideable, let alone crafted according to the machine perfection I've witnessed on prior occasions. Frankly, the swell looks almost "out of control," on the verge of overwhelming the reef's ability to reliably shape the waves. Rather than arrive from the usual north or northeast angle, the swell shows more northwest, making the waves hit the reef head on, without the benefit of a tapering slant. I consider even venturing outside the boat in such conditions a worthy accomplishment, and resent Riley's challenge.

"This isn't a surf contest," I reply. "Nobody's gonna push me into a wave I don't want."

"Of course it's a contest," Riley retorts. "That's what life is. The sooner you realize that, the sooner you'll overcome your mediocrity. This is the real deal—the next level, if you prefer."

Irked by Riley's praise of social Darwinism, which only heightens my sense of vulnerability, I drop the conversation and ponder my predicament. Within minutes, I doubt the wisdom of my scheme. The horizon peels upward, and Brobdingnagian shadows fill the void. When Riley begins a swift paddle seaward, my doubt inspires a frantic effort to place as much distance between myself and the impact zone as possible. The first wave, a lesser villain in a malevolent duo, serves an appetizer of the fear that the second wave offers as a main dish. Responding to the urgency of the situation, the 7'5" provides a burst of paddle power. I dodge the first assault with enough comfort to marvel at the way the wave's glassy wall frames a reflection of jungle peaks far shoreward. The second wave, scorning any such aesthetic appreciation, sucks so much water up its face that warbles snake

191

from trough to crest. A mutant double lip, ignorant of Palikir's reputation for sculpted form, crowns the monstrosity, projects forward, and looks fully intent upon crushing our heads. Guided by preservation instincts emanating from the most reptilian portion of our brains, we claw diagonally up the vertical wall, evade the lip, and descend breathless over the back. Frustrated with the loss of its prey, the wave hurls its fury toward the reef.

"How should a real surfer respond to THAT?" I inquire. The possibility that the swell might increase, unleashing bigger rogues, rattles my mind.

"Wave selection," Riley says breathlessly. "We adhere to the principle of wave selection."

After several minutes, reassured by the absence of further freaks, we drift back to the takeoff zone, where a procession of triple overhead "freight trains" steams down the reef. Occasionally, a daunting yet quite rideable sample of Palikir perfection arrives from a more northerly angle, offering an amiable invitation that stands in contrast to the hostile energy of the westerly walls. Frequently, such tempting invitations precede a horizon-busting set that makes us scramble for safety. In such fashion do the elements toy with us. During this time, not a breath of wind stirs the air, nor do any rays of comforting sun penetrate the overcast. No creature, whether winged or finned, ventures near. The ordinary expressions of nature remain sheltered while the Earth's primordial antagonism—a battle between water and land—transpires along Pohnpei's reefs.

Eventually, a wave comes along that even my caution-fogged eyes recognize as a gift. A beauty queen rising from a parade of ogres, it postures perfectly, baring a graceful sloping shoulder to entice our interest. As a lip puckers along the crest, we both turn to paddle, but being lighter, I exert more speed from the 7'5" and soon gain momentum down the wave. Riley backs out and hoots me onward, a gesture that obligates me to re-evaluate my silly scheme of only pretending to catch waves. Fearing the string of expletives that will no doubt assault my ears should I back out, I paddle a few extra strokes to boost my speed, stand as the 7"5" tracks down the face, and feel my stomach swoon as the wave suddenly jacks, adding several feet to its already lofty proportions. Battling acrophobia, my mind replays a desperate mantra: "don't fall!" Thankfully, the 7"5" shows all the vigor of a racehorse glorying in the purpose to which it was born. Spurred on by the clamorous cascade, it flies across the looming sections, gouging a silver streak like a provocative grafitero. Abandoned in that streak lies any allegiance I have to the principles of good surfing. Driving for the channel, I ignore

193

all opportunities to turn hard off the bottom or ride close to the curl. Instead, my stance stink-bug wide, I seek only to maintain the stability of my balance, and let the semi-gun bolt me to safety. In this manner I survive, rather than surf, and when the grand sample of Pacific power exhausts itself over the coral crags of the shallows, relief washes over my muscles, but my thoughts remain tense.

Bobbing alongside the mooring buoy a short paddle seaward, the boat offers a reprieve, and I feel inclined to take a break from the morning's drama. Against my inclination, an imaginary voice, emanating from the 7'5", sounds in my mind: "Let's do that again! Let's feel some more of that power!" Comically, the board seems to speak with Riley's voice, and I direct my gaze back to the takeoff zone, where my companion bobs, a speck on the swells.

There exists a certain class of surfer for whom the sight of big waves—waves that could snap a surfboard (or a spine) like a twig—gives rise not to alarm but excitement. For such surfers, fun occurs only in conditions that send most people scurrying for the safety of solid ground. The attendant hazards of big waves— turbulent hold-downs that make a surfer cling with aching lungs to that last molecule of air, pile-driving impacts that break ribs or dislocate shoulders, strength-sapping swims in search of a lost board—may cause such a surfer to flinch, but not to flee.

On New Year's Day at Palikir Pass, I opt to flee.

With humble clarity, I reconfirm the truth briefly held at bay by Riley's prodding and the confidence-boosting speed of the 7'5": the conditions, quite simply, are out of my league. Once recognized, this truth summons other unnerving details, such as our isolation from anyone who might render assistance, and the unsavory prospect of letting the island's poorly-equipped hospital treat any injuries we might incur. I begin to think that our New Year's adventure, far from a simple surf session, represents a hubristic challenge to the elements. Paranoia resurrected, I decide that we should exit the water, and soon. With haste born of my new resolve, I paddle back to the takeoff zone to present my arguments.

Before I can proceed a dozen strokes, the swell delivers an argument more forceful than any I can articulate. Beyond the takeoff zone, a brooding shadow signals another ill-mannered set. Riley paddles to greet it and then, to my jaw-dropping surprise, angles for the maw of the beast. Not so much a wave as a grey Mountain of Death, projecting terror from the liquid scythe of its summit, the beast aspires to rogue status beyond the measure of its predecessors.

"Are you crazy?" I holler. "Not that wave!"

Perhaps seeing an angle visible only to him, Riley digs hard to gain forward momentum, and commits to a late take-off that, if performed successfully, could qualify for inclusion in the annals of surf-lore. Unfortunately, late proves *too* late; the wave punishes Riley's bravado with a vertical lurch that launches both board and rider into the air. Somehow, Riley manages to reconnect with his board, but lands broadside to the wave and digs a rail. The board stalls. Flung from his board, Riley hurtles forward, descends to the wave's nether regions, and endures a sepulchral tour of Palikir's coral catacombs. Several moments later, dragged well toward the shallows by the tumult, the board rises from the froth, but an agonizing period of doubt passes before its rider also emerges, gasping for breath with desperate lungs. Thankfully, no further rogues approach, and I paddle toward the scene of the drubbing to offer assistance. Recovering his strength, Riley clambers atop his board and strokes for the safety of the channel.

"I've got a bad feeling about this swell," I say, my tone mirroring the grey, seething mood of the elements.

Still dazed from his pummeling, my companion tilts an

ear and coughs. "Huh?" he says hoarsely, sputtering seawater.

"You got lucky just now," I reply. "What if another rogue had followed the one you took? You could have faced a two-wave hold-down."

Riley makes no reply, but his paddling loses some enthusiasm. I sense an opportunity to press my concerns.

"For all we know the swell is still building, and the north-westerly angle is already creating a lot of mutant sets," I say. "Sooner or later one of them is going to catch us inside, break our leashes or boards, and leave us with no choice but a long swim through sharky water. I don't like that choice, so I'm heading to the boat." The phrase "sharky water" comes somewhat as an afterthought, but I soon congratulate myself on its dramatic effect. Though his waterman's heart remains ambitious, Riley now ponders the one thing—sharks—sure to elicit caution in him. As I recall from prior conversations on the subject, Riley hates sharks.

Riley glowers at me, as though my use of the "S"-word represents a form of unsportsmanlike conduct. Reluctantly, he follows me to the boat, his mind no doubt pondering which expletive best fits my cowardice.

For my part, expletives bother me less than the nagging sixth-sense that fills my head with impending doom. Indeed, upon reaching the boat, we find the water roiled by strange eddies and currents. The surge of passing swells causes the boat to pitch wildly, straining against its tether like an animal sensing danger to which its owner remains oblivious.

"I've got a bad feeling about this swell," I reiterate, grabbing the skiff's rail to maintain my balance.

The wild bucking of the boat makes Riley re-think our mooring. Foregoing his usual after-surf indulgence of snacks and beer, he stows the surfboards, starts the motor, and deftly unties the mooring line. Steering for the lagoon, we motor quickly through the cross currents. I let my gaze follow our bubbly wake back to the reef-line and the grey hostility beyond. What greets my eyes renders me momentarily speechless, and I point frantically seaward. A fugitive from the Jurassic Age, the looming shadow seems spawned by some nefarious alliance of sea and sky; even the clouds appear to lend their grey bellies to its crest. In an expression of disdain for the trinkets of humanity, the wave lurches out of the depths and swallows the mooring buoy, which submerges like a red pill into a liquid stomach. Spared by a fortuitous combination of premonition and luck, we stare at the carnage, and return to the harbor, the meek drone of the outboard offering a soundtrack appropriate to our deflated egos.

The next day, the swell reaches a crescendo. Having reduced us to spectators, the surf gods now arrange a spell of glorious weather, intended to advertise the power of the sea to anyone who might dare challenge it. Abundant sunshine illuminates the aquatic stage, and a light trade wind dissipates the mist that previously clung to the reef-line, allowing an unfettered view of a swell parade extending to the horizon. From the hilltop parking lot of Club Cupid, we obtain a panoramic vista, and train binocular-enhanced gazes at the reef passes. Neither of us voices an estimate of the wave size, but the sight of surf regularly dwarfing the lighthouse (situated on a promontory of reef seaward from the airport) verifies the massive stature of the swell.

"Phe-no-me-nal," Riley says, drawing out the syllables for dramatic effect. "That's the word for this swell. I can't wait to see what the Guam guys do with it. They should arrive on today's flight."

"The Guam guys?" I query.

"Nelson and Dale"

Riley waxes poetic as he describes the exploits of Nelson, an American expat living on Guam and known for occasional surf explorations through the FSM. One day the previous winter, Nelson proved himself a master of serendipity, arriving on

197

Pohnpei just in time to greet a new swell, and then magically catching the wave of the season as if by appointment pre-arranged.

"He caught the kind of fantasy wave we might have drawn on our notebooks as teenagers," Riley recalls. "He rode it along the entire reef, merging his energy with its energy, slotted in a translucent barrel the whole time—never even got his hair wet. The incredible thing was where he took off—way up the reef, even beyond the outside corner, where most surfers wouldn't even think to go. He didn't so much catch the wave as the wave came to him."

"Awesome," I say, unused to hearing Riley speak in such terms.

"Imagine what a guy like that could do in a swell like this."

My imaginings sketch out a sort of shao-lin priest of the sea, his board glossed not by resin but by enlightenment, able to commune with waves beyond the scope of mortal surfers. When I wonder what inspiration such a surfer might provide for someone like me, my imaginings turn to nightmares that vary in detail but generally relate to the topic of Confronting Big Waves and Drowning.

The next day finds me standing resolute in Riley's driveway, my nightmares trumped by curiosity about the "Guam guys." Nelson, his lean build honed for aerobic efficiency, wears ordinary surf trunks rather than shao-lin robes, but exudes an extraordinary confidence as he loads surf gear into the boat. Dale, built like a fireplug, looks more delighted than deterred by my recollection of the rogue sets that roiled Palikir on New Year's Day.

At a word from Riley we hitch the boat trailer to the truck and finalize our departure. As we roll out into the street, the dogs chase after us, hearing in our clatter an occasion for play. Nipping alternately at each other's tails and the trailer tires, they provide a bit of comic relief, and for the first time in two days I feel a smile crease my cheeks. Indeed, the day offers much to smile about— tropic sun tempered by a moist breeze, postcard peaks kissed by scudding clouds. Further down the street, brown kids chase a soccer ball, their revelry an image of innocent fun.

After boating out to the reef, we find the waves coming from a benign northerly angle, as if the swell, regretting its earlier tantrum, now wished to convey a more conciliatory demeanor. The swell's northerly angle allows the reef to exert a dramatic tapering effect on the waves. Accordingly, we arrive at Palikir to find adrenaline-racing perfection. I recall Nelson's reputation as a master of serendipity, and think that someone interested in big, perfect waves couldn't have arranged things better, timing his arrival to find the swell at its most pristine. Yet despite its newfound perfection, the swell remains big, and I can't quite shake my thoughts of doom and gloom.

A particularly thick wave unloads across the reef. Nelson and Dale—big-game hunters assessing their quarry—stare it down. The confident comrades help Riley drop anchor and, without a second glance at the conditions, brandish their equipment: nondescript pintail thrusters whose dents and bruises attest to prior battles challenged and survived.

Once in the water, Nelson and Dale put on a clinic that takes the bite, if not the bark, from my big-wave fears. Pile dives on to the reef? No problem, Dale demonstrates, as he nonchalantly flings himself into the curl of a triple-overhead "bomb," gets axed by the lip, and emerges from the rinse cycle with reef-scrapes etched red upon his back. His fireplug stature absorbing aquatic body blows, Dale treats the waves as adversaries in a gladiatorial contest. Each ride leads to some deeper understanding of his foe, until at last the sea submits to his persistence and he tames a wild barrel that tosses around him like

Pristine Palikir, showing the tapering effect of a more benign northerly angle. Though a bit blurry, this photo remains a favorite from my collection, conveying Palikir's immaculate symmetry better than words can relate. If I had to condense my Micronesian experience into one quintessential moment, this would be it: Palikir Pass, winter 1999-2000, before the hype, before the gold rush, a state of mind as much as a place on the map.

a blue mane. When he emerges, gliding in triumph over the back of the wave, accolades of foam crown his shoulders.

"Tubemaster McShane!" Riley exclaims. The presence of surfers who can push him to the next level ignites his enthusiasm.

In contrast to Dale, Nelson follows a zen-like patience, drifting calmly up the reef while alluring set waves pass him by. Eventually, a deepening shadow sets him in motion, and he drops into a wave that initially looks no better than a close-out. Then, his board a blur of speed, he draws such a smooth line that we all watch transfixed. Like a canvas transformed by an artist's brush into a thing of beauty, the wave responds to Nelson's board strokes, acquiring a form perhaps derived from Nelson's imagination. When Nelson turns vertically off the top, the pitching lip relents, providing just the right amount of liquid coping; when Nelson drives for the tube, the spinning barrel encases his silhouette in blue crystal—an archetypal image of surf nirvana, where Nelson lingers with casual aplomb, as though the idea of surf nirvana originated with him.

Such scenes give me the impression of paddling into a surf movie, and through the course of the afternoon, Nelson and Dale, star performers, shine in the limelight of Palikir's tubes. The two wave warriors play their roles without fanfare, as though their tube-riding prowess makes them privy to visions which render all else trivial. Comfortable in my supporting role, I remain on the periphery, making cameo appearances upon the humbler set waves. When Riley successfully stalks some limelight of his own, I eventually sidle my way to the main peak.

"Well Jacques. . .did you finally decide to put away your clown suit?" Riley prods.

The comment elicits some teasing laughter, but Nelson offers a sympathetic glance. "You gotta realize it's all psychological," Nelson advises. "That's the key to riding waves like these. At the intersection of the idiotic and the intrepid, you'll find a sweet spot where you glide with confidence. In the sweet spot, you can take a wave on the head, get pummeled, and realize *it's not that bad*."

Dale nods his agreement but offers an editorial amendment. "I'll be hurting tomorrow" he says, his reef scrapes a fiery red. "But if you wanna play, you gotta pay."

The boys hoot their agreement, as if hearing in Dale's words the slogan of a big wave brotherhood. So might the bleating of sacrificial lambs sound to the ears of the surf gods.

Perhaps interpreting our enthusiasm as hubristic disrespect, the surf gods now strike. A single rogue wave, treating our clustered assembly as an opportunity to inflict maximum damage, resurrects the fury of New Year's Day. The horizon disappears behind the wave's looming crest, while a black hole trough opens a chasm in the sea, sucking the five of us toward our doom.

"Macker!" Nelson yells, shoulders rippling as he sprint-paddles for deep water. Riley and Dale, nearest the channel, sport an even chance of scaling the wave's unbroken shoulder. Nelson, facing longer odds, aims to punch his board through the underside of the lip. Caught fully in the impact zone, I watch the axe descend on my head, and pray for the "sweet spot" of confidence that, according to Nelson, awaits those who place themselves at the intersection of the idiotic and the intrepid.

Guided by an instinctive sense that I should cling to my board at all costs, I attempt a duck-dive. Amazingly, my efforts meet little resistance—at first. Though the impact of the lip resonates like a depth charge, I evade the bulk of the whitewater explosion. Lofted to the surface on the backs of silver bubbles, I briefly glimpse sky and clouds. Then, enveloped by a sickening weightlessness, I plunge backwards, my board a tombstone masquerading as foam and fiberglass. Nevertheless, I maintain my instinctive grip, though my board and I cartwheel twice in our backwards descent to the depths, seemingly spun for amusement by giant liquid fingers. A blast of turbulence, laden with aqueous animosity, jolts my board from my grasp and pummels me into the dismal depths, where pincers of pressure squeeze my eardrums and strain my lungs. Above me, glimmering amid the wave's foamy aftermath, shards of gold mark the sunlit world, but I reach for them in vain, my upward progress thwarted by the inept flagella of my writhing limbs. My board, caught by the cascade, drags me by the leash further into darkness, where I simply close my eyes and resign myself to fate. Finally, reduced to a feeble lump of weak will and small ambition, I rise to the surface, resembling the waterlogged detritus of something chewed up and spit out by the sea. Gasping in the manner of the nearly-drowned, I retrieve my board and sag over the rails.

"Well, that wasn't so bad!" Nelson opines. "Just imagine—if you'd only been a bit further out, you could have ridden that one. The barrel was epic!"

*   *   *

Excerpt from a Diary, February 2000:

The varied superlatives of surf slang—"epic," "all time," "on fire," "going off," etc.—hint at, but don't fully convey, the degree of perfection that characterizes the surfing experience in Pohnpei during January and February of the year 2000. Disciples of the swell, Riley and I find in Palikir's temple a vision of the sublime. We surf days of silver smooth water, when the approaching swells, like glass stained with the colors of the reef, resemble windows opening into the soul of the sea. On other days, soft trade winds lift from the wave crests a mist like nectar blown from flowers. Mesmerized by the wonders of the wave garden, we linger in a stupor that we call "blue bliss."

     Eventually, one February afternoon, my time in the temple leads me to the chamber of full devotion, and I find myself ensconced in a spinning tunnel of translucent blue, pursued by the voice of the cosmos, seeking an exit to a world seemingly illuminated by a different sun. When I emerge, glistening with mist, I wonder if the course of my life had been designed to place me on that particular wave at that particular time, as if the resulting communion meant something significant to the universe.

204

Chapter 10: A Moonlight Meditation

By March the run of surf fades to dribbles and disappears altogether. Deprived of my Blue Bliss, I decompress in the routine of professional life. Unfortunately, in an island climate ruled by lassitude and decay, the very idea of professional routine represents a challenge to the natural order. The path of productivity, however seriously embarked upon, inevitably descends into thickets of distraction. In my case, the thickets come in the form of neighborhood drama, and arise just when I attempt to tackle the pile of un-graded papers on my desk.

Chips, the Linskey's dog, never expressed any ambition greater than the typical canine endeavors of eating and napping. In light of this, news of his disappearance roils Fern Cove. Some say the scent of a female in heat lured him from his porch. Others contend he joined ranks with a pack of strays recently seen sniffing refuse heaps in distant villages. When even a fisherman's feast—a celebration prompted by the exploits of a Fern Cove neighbor, whose sportfishing expedition returned in triumph with a large black marlin—fails to conjure the canine, we succumb to rumors of a darker hue: dog eaters, we speculate, purloined the pooch. Our fear that Chips might simmer in a stewpot provides a call to action. The matter gains added emotion when we see Penelope, the Linskey's third grade daughter, sitting despondently by the dog's water bowl. Let the islanders eat their own dogs, we reason—but let them face justice when they threaten an American family's well-loved pet. An ex-pat posse, we mobilize search parties and set off in a blaze of righteous indignation.

Driving alone on the southbound road, I find the banner of justice torn by the thorns of practicality. The requirements of the search—peering into roadside yards and clumps of foliage while avoiding oncoming traffic, calling Chip's name repeatedly but to no avail, accelerating toward four legged apparitions that from a distance look like dogs but upon closer inspection resolve into tricks of light and shadow—convey the slim odds of finding a lost dog amid Pohnpei's tropical lushness. Worse, the enterprise entails a certain amount of risk, as I discover in a moment of near disaster. Rounding a blind curve, I peer a little too intently at a trick of light and shadow, and not intently enough at the road, a breach of driving protocol that places me in a near-collision with

Fisherman's feast. A big catch often prompted a communal culinary event, drawing neighbors and tag-alongs, both local and ex-pat, from the surrounding area.

a U.S. Army Humvee parked upon the roadside. A frantic "watch out!" — uttered in the shrill tone of a female voice raised in alarm — prods me to brake, swerve, and skid to an ignominious halt, my sedan's front fender mired in bushes. The maneuver raises a cloud of dust, which sends a pair of women into a bout of gagging, eye-rubbing, and clothes-brushing. The dust dissipates, and the women — an attractive duo in their late twenties — step away from the Humvee, in whose lee they had taken shelter.

"Great," says the taller of the pair. Dressed in cammo fatigues, she wears a short-billed cap bearing the insignia of a lieutenant. "First, the Humvee breaks down, and now my uniform gets a dust bath."

"Sorry," I reply, silently critical of the wisdom that led them to park the Humvee on a blind curve. "I'm looking for a lost dog." The information casts me in a moral light, even if it doesn't defend my driving, and I see the hint of a smile soften the lieutenant's stern demeanor.

"Well, maybe you've found two lost ladies," the lieutenant sighs. "We really need some help."

Her companion, wafting a scent of patchouli from bracelet-adorned wrists, regards the lieutenant with a cynical expression, which she then turns on me. "I'm not a lady and I don't need help. But I'll accept cooperative assistance, freely given," she clarifies.

"Please, Sis," the lieutenant admonishes. "Let me handle this."

"I'm an English teacher, not a mechanic," I say, still unsure if I want to get involved.

"The guys back at camp can fix our vehicle," the lieutenant says. "However, I can't raise them on the radio. The island topography blocks our signals."

"Camp?" I ask.

"The C.A.T. Camp. We're beyond Keprohi Falls, where

210

the road curves along the southern coast." Seeing my continued confusion, the Lieutenant explains further. "C.A.T. stands for Civic Action Team. We're a good-will special force, providing medical care and infrastructure assistance for isolated island communities."

The explanation wins me over completely. How could I refuse to help a good-will special force? "I'll do what I can," I reply.

After placing some flares in the road, we begin our journey to the southern shore. At first, I continue my dog search with genuine effort, and enlist the assistance of my new passengers. Soon, however, my eyes linger less on roadside yards and linger longer on the svelte figures seated in my car. In part, these glances result from curiosity about the women's behavioral quirks: both bite their nails and twitch their noses as a nervous tic. Mostly, though, the glances result from that lustful mind-set with which men too long deprived of female companionship will eye the female form. Lest they suspect my prurient mind, I distract my companions with small talk.

"Do you ladies have names?"

"I'm Carly," the lieutenant says. "The frowning face in back belongs to my sister. Becky's visiting here before flying on to Australia, where she plans to volunteer on an organic farm." The lieutenant presents this in a tone of disdain, as though she doesn't approve of the plan.

I introduce myself and ask why Becky frowns.

"She hates the term 'lady.' She considers it politically oppressive."

"Politically oppressive?" I inquire, marveling how my attempt at small talk morphed into serious conversation.

"Don't worry. Becky didn't come here to embroil people in arguments, right Beck?" Carly says, turning to cast a pleading glance at her sister.

"Don't talk to me that way," Becky says. "Just because you don't take my ideas seriously doesn't mean you have to mock them in front of others."

"Come on, Becky. I take you seriously. I just think there's a time and place for things."

"If you took my ideas seriously, you'd explain them seriously. I don't approve of the word 'lady' because I don't approve of the patriarchal power structure that created the concept of ladies. Maybe if you spent more time reading French feminism, you'd understand. Like me, you would prefer linguistically-subversive labels, such as--"

"Yeah, I know. W-O-M-Y-N," the Lieutenant interrupts, spelling the term with mock enunciation. "Unfortunately, there wasn't much feminism on the curriculum at West Point."

"Well, you know what I think of West Point, and the military in general."

Engrossed in their sibling feud, the sisters pay little attention to me. Accordingly, I content myself with a voyeuristic assessment of their personalities, gleaned from carefully scrutinized bits of conversation. Becky, protester of patriarchy, fresh from an Asian backpacking trek that left her "karmically aware and devoted to world happiness," portrays herself as Carly's Bohemian alter ego, free from the shackles of career, status, and money. Carly, confident commander and pursuer of power, harbors that sense of accomplishment provided by a steady paycheck and a generous benefit package. In the manner of siblings long used to rivalry, the sisters know which slings and arrows best exploit each other's vulnerabilities.

"You're just a wayward dreamer," Carly accuses.

"At least I have the courage to dream," Becky replies. "You have your rank, but I have my experiences."

"That and a dollar will get you a cup of coffee," Carly retorts.

The steamy Southeast coast. Threading between rugged slopes and the lapping lagoon, the road pushes into a jungle hinterland.

Apropos to the animosity, intermittent drafts of hot air, like the exhalations of some restive dragon, waft through the windows, carrying an aroma of dust and overheated foliage. Heat mirages—ghostly puddles that turn to potholes and ruts as we approach—shimmer on the road. Sagging slopes cower from the light, cloistered behind the green robes of the jungle canopy. Charlotte massages her temples and forehead. "I think this heat is starting to give me a headache," she mutters.

"Don't blame the heat," Becky says. "Blame your mind-body connection. You need to restore the balance of your chakras."

"I'd prefer two aspirin and an air-conditioned room," Carly replies.

"Join me tonight for full-moon meditation. Let the light of the silver orb bring alignment with Shambala."

Though Carly seems to cringe, something in Becky's soft syllables makes the heat less hot and my sweat less sticky. To my mind comes a mental image of an enormous full moon, birthed from the sea to bring healing from the ravages of the sun. I hold on to the thought as I navigate the remainder of the road to the southern shore.

Situated in a grassy clearing, the C.A.T. camp asserts a military order into the jungle chaos. Single story buildings, an array of satellite dishes and radio antennae, and corrugated metal sheds (one with an awning shading a jeep) comprise an outpost of modernity, where predictable angles and ruler edges offer an industrious comfort.

When we pull into the clearing, we find the ruler edges a scene for unruly behavior, as exemplified by the duo of soldiers who, apparently devolving to schoolyard bullies, pin one of their undersized comrades belly-down on the lawn and pull his underwear up his back, completing the act of torture known to playground primitives as a "wedgie." The arrival of my sedan puts a halt to their antics. Recognizing the lieutenant, the soldiers stand and brush the grass from their shirts.

"Stillman," the lieutenant orders, "go fetch the sergeant. Tell him the Humvee broke down again."

One of the soldiers trots off in compliance, while the wedgie victim picks himself off the grass, readjusts his underwear and sulks away toward one of the buildings. The remaining soldier eyes me with the suspicion of a guard eager to hone security skills long practiced but seldom used.

"Relax, Carter," the lieutenant says. "Jacques works as an English professor at the College. Anyway, we could all use a cold drink. I don't know about my sister, but I'm about to wilt." From the hiss she adds to the word "sister," I infer their feud still simmers.

Carter puts his suspicions on hold and shuffles off to procure refreshment.

"My guys get a little protective," the lieutenant explains apologetically.

"If they do, it's your fault," Becky remarks. "Telling them you're about to wilt only inspires their masculine instinct. Why not get your own drink? The fridge isn't hard to find." In a huff, Becky follows the soldiers indoors.

News of the broken-down Humvee ensures that displeasure spreads beyond the quarreling sisters. Wearing the scowl of a man who finds his well-orchestrated day disrupted by the incompetence of others, the sergeant emerges into the sunlight and steps grudgingly toward the lieutenant, his pace modulated more by deference to her rank than by enthusiasm to say hello. Thick shouldered, with perspiration lending a shine to his bald head, the sergeant projects the persona of Mr. Clean, and even assumes the same cross-armed posture, although instead of Mr. Clean's iconic white T-shirt, he wears an apron dotted with cooking splatter.

"So," he says, eyeing me coolly before taking aim at the lieutenant, "I hear you're having problems with the Humvee." The phrase "you're having problems" seems crafted to place the matter in the lieutenant's domain of responsibility.

"Unfortunately, yes," she says. "I know it's frustrating, considering all the work you put into that vehicle just last week."

"I just got my chili on the stove," the sergeant protests, pointing to his apron.

"Let's focus on priorities," the lieutenant advises. "We've got some valuable government property abandoned by the roadside. Letting it remain there doesn't reflect well on the Army or our mission."

"I guess if you put it *that* way," the sergeant sighs. He orders a soldier to load the toolbox into the jeep. As he unties his apron, the sodas arrive for the lieutenant and me. No doubt perceiving some injustice in the circumstances which require him to work while others relax, the sergeant fixes us in a glare of resentment.

Unmoved by the sergeant's grumblings, the lieutenant, smiling sweetly, addresses me. "Thank you for the lift, Jacques. I understand if you want to resume the dog-search. However, the manner-minded damsel in me wants to invite you to dinner. A college professor like you would give our table a conversational upgrade."

Still within earshot, the sergeant bristles, forearm muscles flexing.

I ponder a return to the road, and the hot, dusty, likely fruitless dog-hunt. Then, enjoying the tingle of soda on my tongue, I picture relaxing in the comfort of the C.A.T. camp's air-conditioned quarters. Hearing the lieutenant refer to me as a "professor" who could provide a "conversational upgrade" flatters my ego. I accept the invitation, and the lieutenant, taking me by the arm, escorts me toward the main building. As we walk, barbs of ill-will, the jealous resentment of an alpha-male feeling under-appreciated, bore into my back.

"Enjoy your soda," the sergeant growls, unsheathing sarcasm.

The lieutenant leads me out of the heat and into the living quarters. A smell of simmering spices wafts around us.

"It's the sergeant's recipe," she explains, seeing me inhale the aroma. She beckons me to a table, where we relish the air-conditioning and the remainder of our sodas. "I apologize for all that bickering in the car. My sister and I must have put you in an uncomfortable situation," she says. "We never really got along well, and I haven't seen her in years. We were on our way back from brunch at the Village Hotel when the Humvee broke down."

"No need for apologies," I say. "I don't mind uncomfortable situations when they involve such lovely damsels as yourselves."

"You're kind—but don't let Becky hear you put it that way! She might not approve of your word choice." Carly makes a comedic show of looking over her shoulder, as though her sister might lurk nearby. She sips her soda, sighs, and massages her forehead. "I've got a throbbing headache," she says. "I'm going to lie down for a bit. Just make yourself at home and I'll send someone in to look after the chili."

In the wake of her departure, the chili pot bubbles and burps. Soon, footsteps approach. I recognize the new chef, Edwards (or so the name patch on his uniform indicates), as the sulking soldier who suffered the wedgie on the lawn. He grunts a greeting without making eye contact and wears a sullen expression that makes me think his assignment to chili duty comprises just one item on a long list of complaints. As an awkward silence passes between us, he peers into the chili kettle, evaluating its contents according to some private metric of broth and beans that convinces him to grab a jar of red paste from the fridge and spoon some into the kettle.

"Smells fantastic," I say, making an attempt at sociability.

Edwards paces, stares out the window, and eventually mumbles a reply. "I can't stand the stuff myself."

"Oh," I say, unsure how to respond.

Edwards turns to face me, cracks his knuckles, and leans his weight against the chair vacated by the lieutenant. The uneasy silence resumes, until Edwards breaks it with a statement whose tone straddles interrogation and conversation.

"So, I hear yer a college perfessor."

"I prefer the term 'instructor,'" I say, curious if Edwards' mispronunciation resulted from intention or just a back-woods upbringing. "To me, the term 'professor' applies to faculty with a Ph.D."

"You ain't got a Ph.D?"

"No. I have a Master's degree." My willingness to downplay my rank puts Edwards a bit more at ease, and he settles into the chair, though his expression conveys a remnant of mistrust.

"Master's degree, huh. . .still, I bet that took a lot of schoolin'. . .I bet folks give you some respect."

I shrug, picturing my clownish students and their habit of spitting betel-juice out the window during lecture. Then, moved to introspection, I wax philosophical about my career choice, and offer some commentary that seems inspired in its crafting but turns to platitude upon delivery. "Really, my job isn't about me; it's about the students. If my class gives them a new perspective about the world, I feel I've done something meaningful."

Edwards' eyes retain a downcast vacuity. Remembering a courteous guest sings the praises of his host, I shift the attention to him. "You must get a similar thrill from your work with the C.A.T. team," I suggest. "In the big picture, our jobs have the same goal: improving life for the islanders."

Edwards sighs, his downcast eyes signaling a troubled mind. "My life in the Army is pretty much a waste of time," he informs me. "You know what the letters P.F.C. mean?"

"Private First Class?" I venture

"Nah," Edwards smirks. "They mean Professional Floor Cleaner."

"You can't really mean that," I console. "Surely your service has value others appreciate."

With a shrug that suggests my civilian sensibilities couldn't possibly understand the depth of his suffering, Edwards deflects my well-meant boosterism. "The Army done screwed me over," he asserts.

Convinced that Edwards needs solitude more than solace, I excuse myself and explore beyond the kitchen. Despite Edward's grievances, the building conveys a spit-and-polish atmosphere reflective of the occupants' deference to decorum. Counters and appliances gleam. In the sleeping quarters, bunks stand in formation, and sheets lie taut, tucked in hospital corners. Bathroom surfaces, fragrant with Lysol, boast an immunity to mildew, a notable achievement on an island where humidity and damp surfaces catalyze a fungal plague. Such protocols serve a larger purpose, as indicated by an American flag placed conspicuously upon the living room wall. Sufficiently proportioned to remind visitors of the C.A.T. camp's national allegiance, the flag infuses a patriotic esprit de corps into the premises.

Walking past a storage room, I find esprit de corps prods more than patriotism. By a partly open window, two soldiers — the pair who inflicted the wedgie on Edwards — peer out at the lawn as though conducting some mission of surveillance. Curious, I step toward them, and a creak in the floor signals my presence. The soldiers face me, grin conspiratorially, and return to their gazing.

"Now she's really putting on a show," one says.

"Hey man, take a look," says the other, waving me alongside.

I recognize a graceful figure on the lawn: Becky, posed upon a yoga mat, a skimpy bikini her only deference to modesty. Arms behind her head, she pushes her spine into an arch, offering her navel in supplication to the sky. Juxtaposed against the jungle background, she resembles a forest nymph, delighting in the sensations of an untainted Earth. Becky arches her spine to its full extent, and sunlight spills over her, pooling upon her torso with risqué refulgence.

Catcalls and whistles erupt from the soldiers and draw attention to our voyeurism. Embarrassed, I retreat into the shadows, but not before Becky, startled out of her pose, rewards our appreciation with a middle finger gesture. My companions, full of esprit de corps, laugh, slap high-fives, and slink away.

Becky approaches the window, and looks into the room the way a zoo visitor might look at an animal in an enclosure. "Well, Jacques," she says, her scowl an indictment of the male psyche, "I wouldn't have figured you for a Peeping Tom."

"Peeping Tom?" I protest, seeking to downplay my role in the incident. "Really, I had no idea. . ."

"Did you enjoy the view?" Becky prods. "I have a much better body than my sister. That's why she resents me so much."

"I wasn't trying to make a comparison," I assure her. "Really, I just happened to be walking by when —"

"Sure. . . you happened to be walking by when those meatheads invited you to a peep show. I shouldn't be surprised. This place is overflowing with right-body energy. No wonder my sister suffers from headaches."

"Right-body energy?"

"The right-body is the sun-side orientation which gives rise to the masculine mind. The sergeant brims with it. In fact, he

220

pretty much epitomizes the affliction of hyper-masculinity. When men don't understand their bodies, they don't understand their connection to the Earth. The result is a constant, smoldering anger."

"What can we do?"

"Develop left-body awareness. The left body orients to the moon, and a more feminine, nurturing energy."

"What is that like?"

"You probably wouldn't understand."

"Well, I try to keep an open mind about things."

"In that case, come out here and I'll try to show you."

I exit the room, find a doorway to the lawn, and stagger through the sunlight to where Becky stands serene on her yoga mat.

"I'm going to lead us through Utkata Konasana, also known as Goddess Pose," Becky says. "It helps channel the lunar feminine."

Following Becky's example, I widen my stance so that my knees, when bent, center a vertical line above my ankles. I then hinge my feet about 45 degrees in opposite directions, giving my legs and knees an outward flare. Keeping my spine straight and head level, I lower my pelvis toward the ground, until my thighs bend almost at right angles to my legs. Becky then tells me to lift my heels, so that I balance on the balls of my feet.

"How does that feel?" Becky asks.

"OK so far," I reply, though a quiver in my quadriceps makes me unsure. "How long do I have to stay like this?"

"About five minutes."

"Five minutes!" I cry, feeling the quiver become a quake.

Inspired by the graceful strength with which Becky holds the pose, I galvanize my glutes and attempt to channel the left-body awareness that Becky described. Instead, after a minute which brings only solar spite and muscular misery, I collapse on

221

the grass.

"I guess I need more practice," I mumble, marveling at the way Becky perseveres through the discomforts I found so daunting.

"It's all in the breath," she says. "Calm breath produces a calm mind. In my mind I'm a lotus sitting on the water, beyond time and space."

Finding enlightenment more elusive than I hoped, I retreat to the living room and a sofa amenable to slouching.

That evening, set free from the oppressive sun, a light air settles on the meadow, silky and comforting. Gleaming beams, emanating from a low-slung moon, coat the grass with an astral marinade. Into this stillness the sergeant returns, riding a ruckus of revved engines and honking horns. Having tamed the insubordinate Humvee, he swaggers into the kitchen, and enjoys a celebratory beer while placing the finishing touches on his chili. Mindful of my manners, I join the C.A.T. team in welcoming him back to camp.

"Well, if it isn't the professor!" he blurts, pronouncing the job title with mock praise. Lifting his beer on high, he steps toward me and drains a zealous gulp from the bottle. "Nice to have a cold drink on a hot day, eh Prof? The heat today reminded me of Iraq during the Gulf War." The comment seems crafted to highlight his sufferings while mocking my leisure, and, in conjunction with his grease smears — black badges of courage left conspicuously upon his forearms — leaves me awkwardly self-conscious, guilty at having spent the afternoon in comparative luxury.

The lieutenant, leaning against a counter, offers a tension-defusing interjection. "Sarge, why don't you get yourself cleaned up? Maybe a shower will help you. . .*relax*."

"Maybe later," he replies. "Right now, it's chili-time!" With a flourish, he lifts the lid off the pot. "Come and get it!"

Bowls in hand, the CAT team lines up, and the sergeant ladles them a serving. When I approach, he puts down the ladle and hands me a bowl already prepared. "I made you a special version," he tells me.

"I hope you didn't go to any trouble on my account," I say.

"Oh, no trouble at all," he says, a glint in his eye.

Once at the table, I take my first bite. The incendiary throb that spreads across my tongue makes me reach instinctively for the nearest water glass.

"Whaddya think" the sergeant asks, eyeing my reaction.

"Sp-sp-spicy," I gasp, the conflagration in my mouth sucking the wind from my lungs. "Remi-mi-minds me of Tabasco."

"Tabasco's for wimps," the sergeant says. "I use wiri-wiri, a South American pepper about sixty times more powerful."

I dread swallowing yet press on for decorum.

"Sarge, you didn't!" the lieutenant exclaims. "Jacques, if you prefer, I'll get you a different bowl."

Savoring a spoonful of chili for dramatic effect, the sergeant grins, apparently pleased with my discomfort. "Shall I summon a medic?" he asks, seeing my flushed cheeks and watery eyes as symptoms of impending incapacitation.

I drain my water glass, my civilian sensibilities wilting before the sergeant's machismo and the firestorm on my palate. As I contemplate the sergeant's acrimonious tone—motivated, I suspect, by jealousy for the hospitality shown me earlier by the lieutenant—the wiri-wiri spreads throughout my mouth, embarking on a campaign of tissue torment that renders me insensate to anything else.

When I regain my senses, I find the attention of the table focused on a new drama: an argument between the sergeant and Becky. I tune in just as a host of expletives clamor behind the sergeant's lips, reform as glottal rage, and emanate as a growl.

"What I can't stand," the sergeant jabs, "are spoiled brats who don't work real jobs. What gives you the freedom to traipse around the world like a lazy hippy, or allows Jacques to study useless poetry? The U.S. military does."

"Ever hear of Gandhi, or Martin Luther King?" Becky ripostes, unfazed by the masculine menace across the table. "They helped humanity without relying on guns or tanks."

"Gandhi? MLK?" the sergeant questions. "Those are 20th century aberrations. History is a saga of armed conflict."

"*His*tory, yes," Becky parries. "You might have a different view if you learned a little *her*story."

"Sounds like hippie nonsense," the sergeant scoffs.

"That's because you celebrate masculine attainments like power and status, so you forget your feminine side," Becky continues. "Not surprisingly, you accept war as a method of conflict resolution. It's the ultimate masculine conditioning."

The sergeant's voice calms, as if Becky's refusal to back down deserves grudging respect. "So you think you've got it all figured out?" he says quietly. "What should we do the next time an African warlord pirates a U.N. food convoy? Sing Kumbaya?"

"If men understood their feminine side, there wouldn't be warlords," Becky answers. "Men are so out of touch with their bodies that they have lost awareness of Mother Earth and respect for her creations. We see the result right here at this table: a silly contest over who can stomach the hottest chili, and a bunch of guys who treat my yoga routine as a peep show."

Laughter, ripe with right-body energy, ripples around the table, booming with particular force from the sergeant's belly.

"Tell me, Sergeant, when was the last time you sought alignment with Shambala?" Becky asks, unfazed by the outburst. "Are you even aware of the moonlight that, as we speak, washes the air with healing?"

Becky's questions seem so incongruous that they thwart an articulate response. Jaw quivering, the sergeant short-circuits, spoon halted mid-way to his mouth.

"Join me in the moonlight meditation," Becky says. She walks behind the table, stands behind the sergeant, and holds his hands. "Breathe with me. Help me awaken your spine and summon healing energy." Lifting the sergeant's hands with her own, she inhales deeply, until their collective fingers meet above the Sergeant's head. "Focus your breath on your pelvic bowl, and the tail bone will activate," Becky instructs.

"Becky, please. . ." the lieutenant pleads.

"Now awaken your heart chakra," Becky advises, bringing their hands to the center of the sergeant's chest. "With your inhale, summon compassion, and with your exhale, release your ego."

"I'm not doing this," the sergeant growls.

"We project ourselves toward the planetary heart," Becky chants. "Toward the great Ashram of Sanat Kumara, toward Shambala. . ."

Inspired by the soft syllables of Becky's voice, my mind conjures a strange juxtaposition. I perceive the sergeant as an expression of angst, propped upon a torso of military muscle. Behind him stands Becky, a figure of silver hues and soft shadows, posed like a Priestess of Apollo. When she touches the sergeant's chest, the military muscles quiver, and a wrinkle in the sergeant's shirt resembles a fissure in a fortress wall. Still smoldering from my purification by pepper, I can't decide if I've witnessed a mystical moment or another wiri-wiri wonder.

"So, what do you think of my sister?" the lieutenant whispers, leaning close to my ear.

"She's quite a gal," I whisper back. Then, sensing a deficiency in my diction, I add a hasty amendment: "I mean—"

"I know," the lieutenant interjects. "W-O-M-Y-N."

Excerpt from a Diary, March 2000:

In the tropics, melancholia comes upon a pastel pillow. Where the hard edges of the world recede into rainbows, one believes that only the most petulant personality could descend into despair. Yet who knows what misgivings, subtle as summer clouds, lie dormant in the heart, only to unexpectedly darken our dreams? A certain slant of light may strike the bathroom mirror and reveal in one's reflection a touch of gray previously unnoticed, rendering dour what once seemed debonair. Canned food may trigger a maudlin mood, in which the memory of the mainland and its epicurean delights makes island life seem hollow and unsatisfying

I think of these things as I consider my colleague Verne Molson. For years he fought a battle with the bottle, keeping his desire for Demon Rum under the cloak of professional demeanor, until one day the cloak unraveled, and Verne abandoned academics for a shadowy booth of a Kolonia bar. There, after a week-long search, college personnel found him, incoherent and half-dead from alcohol poisoning.

Those of us who know him wonder what gave alcohol its final ascendance. Did the prospect of collecting another set of essays, their grievous grammar beyond repair, convince Verne of the futility of his work and drive him to despair?

In my view, alcohol merely provided a conduit, a substance through which deeper demons found expression. A scion of San Francisco, Verne possibly found his metropolitan mind incompatible with expat existence. I speculate that news from the mainland—a friend's publicized promotion, or well-attended wedding—perhaps reminded Verne of his relative isolation and his status as an unknown fish in an irrelevant pond.

Whatever its cause, Verne's unraveling reminds me of my own vulnerability. Publicly, the College restores routine, but privately I wonder: by what threads do we maintain the fabric of our lives? Which threads, finally fraying, cause the fabric to unravel? In the case of Verne Molson, long-time expat and Language Arts colleague, I see a cynical commentary about the way journeys begun in hope may end in heartbreak.

Chapter 11: Floating, Drifting

From Kitti, a remote village on Pohnpei's Southwest shore, the rumors spread, rippling through the syrupy somnolence of early summer. At first, news of the cholera outbreak elicits surprise, born of the presumption that steamship-era diseases pose little risk to an island blessed with modern marvels like internet and satellite T.V. When people learn the details—three dead, dozens sick, and a U.N. medical team issuing quarantine recommendations—the mood turns somber. The closure until further notice of all sakau bars sows panic amongst even the stalwart optimists, and shoppers, adopting a bunker mentality, strip the markets of bottled water and canned goods. College administrators, citing student health protocol, cancel the remaining two weeks of the semester.

The news casts a pall on my ex-pat existence, injecting a dose of third-world reality into my first-world mindset. In a land beset by cholera, academics seem pointless, an impression that leads me to brood darkly on the circumstances of my life. Magnified through a lugubrious lens, the island's minor annoyances maximize their menace. Mosquitoes buzz demonic, their whiny wings wailing like Stukas. Weevil-infested pasta, once tolerated as a culinary curiosity, now represents a pestilential plot. As paranoia renders paradise putrid, I long for the trappings of my former life. In my mind's eye I conjure California: gentle sun, bug-free food, and my ex-fiancée, vibrant in a V-neck blouse. Numbed by nostalgia, I forget the heartache of our breakup, and think that if I could only embrace her again, we might rekindle our passion and forget the pain.

Full of Quixotic hope, I resolve to call my ex-fiancée, eager to hear in the sound of her voice some token that the pieces of my old life remain intact, that to reclaim them I need only board a plane and soar home to the solace of old love and familiar routine. Embarking on a mad dash for the telecom center, I swerve my sedan through the crisis of Kolonia. Blissfully nonchalant about time-zone differentials that render my call a night-time nuisance in Los Angeles, I storm up to the counter and give the clerk the dialing information. Long distance connections whirr and hum, and finally produce a ring. Grasping the handset with a white-knuckle grip, I close my eyes and focus on a memory of my ex, as though fervent desire at my end of the line might produce a positive outcome on the other.

"Hello?" a woman's voice comes through the receiver.

"K-Kate?" I stammer, my voice tripping over my emotions.

"Yes?" she demands.

"It's me—Jacques."

"Jacques? Why are you calling?"

"I wanted to hear your voice."

"Is something wrong? I've had a long day. I was thinking of going to sleep."

"I miss you so much, Kate," I gush. "We can go to therapy. I'll pick up some teaching jobs. Things will—"

"Things will what?" she questions.

"Be different." Like an echo in the wilderness, the phrase dissipates into silence. Through the line comes a rustle of sheets.

"If you feel that way, why are you 6,000 miles away on an island?" Her words accuse as much as inquire, and I sense my romantic hopes foundering on the shoals of old grievance.

"I don't have to be here," I reply. "I can be there, with you. What do you think?"

A ponderous pause fills the line. In the background, a muffled drone, like a radio voice on low volume, sounds intermittently.

"What do I think?" she says finally, a sudden confidence putting an edge in her voice. "I think we should see other people. Haven't you been dating anyone?"

I ponder the question. My bungled attempts at island romance comprise a narrative of concupiscence for which I offer a succinct summary: "Not really."

"Well, I have," she asserts crisply. Her statement acts like a needle upon the bubble of my fantasy, but I cling steadfastly to the receiver, loath to admit the unrequited nature of my feelings.

Amid the silence that fills the line, I again sense the radio voice I noticed earlier. Then, I realize the radio voice comes not from a radio, but a human mouth in the background. Suddenly Kate's last question resonates in my mind. *Haven't you been dating anyone?* Of course she has. . .and she invited him to spend the night.

The epiphany registers as a body blow. Laid bare to the slings and arrows of outrageous fortune, I pulse with a pathos that renders my voice a whimper. Remembering decorum, I clench my teeth and hang up on salvation.

I wander into the afternoon heat and lean against a street-side wall, seeking some bulwark against the feelings of anger, loneliness, and doubt that threaten to render me Jell-O on the pavement. Fortunately, Fate spares me such an indignity, and offers a chance to play Good Samaritan to a duo of passers-by.

"Hey buddy!" a radiant-eyed man greets me. "My wife and I seem a bit lost. Can you give directions to the Crystal Edge dive shop?"

"Crystal Edge?" I reply. "It's not really a dive shop...more like a tour operator."

"Oh, that's what we're searching for," the wife says breathlessly, her red-flushed cheeks symptomatic of one for whom pedestrianism and tropical heat make for an exhausting combination.

"I'm afraid you'll have to search a bit further," I say, and proffer the requested directions. Curiously, instead of proceeding upon the directed route, the couple fix me in their radiant gaze, as if expecting some further outcome desired but not yet achieved. Sweat-stained green T-shirts, bearing lettered logos, wilt upon the couple's chests.

Jarred by my recent emotional distress, I sense more keenly the suffering of others, and my sympathy for the wilting walkers kindles a sudden altruism. "I can drive you, if you like,"

232

I volunteer.

"Oh, we definitely like!" the couple exclaims, hearing in my words an offer more in line with their hopes.

Apparently used to ready hospitality, the couple ambles confidently beside me toward my car. As we proceed, I scrutinize their T-shirts: "Nomadic Normans, Millennium World Tour," they state.

"We're the Nomadic Normans," the woman says, as though the name conveys a celebrity status. "I'm Nancy and this is my husband, Nat."

"I'm Jacques," I reply, gesturing them into my car with a gallant sweep of my arm.

The mundane acts of exchanging introductions, starting the car, and pulling into traffic help restore a sense of normalcy and numb the trauma of my phone conversation. Unfortunately, the respite lasts only a few blocks, and when I slam on the brakes after getting cut off by a motorcycle so overloaded with cargo that it threatens to capsize in the next pothole, my angst erupts. The driver, whose posterior spills in folds off the seat, projects the sort of confidence that comes from a mindless ignorance of road safety and general common sense. Behind him, propped atop a bamboo crate affixed to the bike's luggage rack, a sibling pair cling, grinning like mischievous imps at the traffic behind them. Tongue lolling between the slats of the crate, a dog stares out with doleful gaze. The motorcycle menagerie, one pothole away from disaster, seems to represent the third-world menace I find so irksome.

"How cute!" Nancy Norman exclaims. "What an adorable family!"

"You wouldn't think so if you knew the kids had leprosy and the dog would be roasted for dinner," I deadpan.

Framed by the rearview mirror, shades of shock contort Nancy's face. "What a terrible thought!" Nancy mutters.

233

"Just offering another perspective," I say, indifferent to her indignation.

"Could you keep that perspective to yourself? Nat and I operate on a very delicate frequency and bad thoughts have the potential to disrupt it."

"Honey, calm down," Nat advises. "Jacques kindly offered us a ride. We shouldn't quarrel with him."

"Sorry. I don't mean to quarrel. I just doubt if Jacques really knows whether they will roast the poor dog."

"True enough," I admit. "They might stew it instead."

"Ugh!" Nancy frowns. The motorcycle menagerie veers down a side street, but my angst endures.

Nat chuckles. "I guess you've seen the dark side of paradise, eh?"

"I've lived here over ten months, teaching English at the College. Some days I wish I could just get the hell off this island."

"English teacher, huh?" Nat says. "We better watch our grammar."

"I'll dot my T's and cross my eyes," Nancy mocks, framing a cross-eyed expression in the rear-view mirror.

"So, you've been on this island nearly a year?" Nat queries.

"Yup," I confirm, with a sigh of self-pity.

"Sounds like you're going a little stir-crazy," Nat opines.

"Funny you should say that," I reply. "Just a little while ago I was all ready to pack my bags for California."

"Why don't you?"

"Well, it's not so simple. See, I signed this thing called a teaching contract, and my ex—"

"Interesting," Nat interrupts. "That's very. . .how should I say. . ."

"*Lifestyle 1.0*," Nancy suggests.

"Lifestyle 1.0?" I query.

234

"Contracts, bosses, obligations," Nat explains. "Lifestyle 1.0 denotes a way of life characterized by limitation and boundaries. You live *in a place*. You work *at a job*."

"Sounds familiar," I say.

"It should," Nat says. "It's the operating system by which most people run their lives."

"Is there another operating system?" I ask, feeling like I've swallowed the bait on a well-rehearsed sales pitch.

"Lifestyle 2.0!" Nancy answers.

"Exactly," Nat continues. "A way of life without boundaries. . .Lifestyle 2.0 represents abundance and freedom. Consider Nancy and me, for example. In the time that you've gone stir-crazy on this island, we've toured Southeast Asia, caravanned Australia and New Zealand, and started island-hopping the Pacific."

"We're the Nomadic Normans!" Nancy cheers.

Raised in Los Angeles, a city long known for the promotion of quirky characters, I naturally strain the Norman's dialog through a filter of cynicism. Certain phrases, such as the gimmicky "Lifestyle 2.0," seemingly lifted from the manual of an advertising executive, rank high on my B.S. meter. Nevertheless, the Normans exude a certain ebullience which provides a refreshing distraction from my dark mood. Wondering if perhaps they had arrived in my life to renew my adventuresome spirit, I adopt an open mind.

"Lifestyle 2.0, huh?" I say. "I admit that sounds pretty nice. Where do I sign up?"

"You don't sign up," Nat replies. "You already have all you need. You, me, Nancy—everybody. The resources necessary for Lifestyle 2.0 exist within us. The key is tapping into them."

"How do I do that?" I ask.

"By *shifting frequencies*. Shift your frequency, manifest abundance!"

"A-bun-dance," Nancy echoes, drawing out the middle syllable like a meditative chant.

"See, the mind works like a radio antenna," Nat explains. "People enjoying Lifestyle 2.0 tune in to signals emanating from the universe. When they want something, they shift frequencies, and—badda-bing, badda-boom—the universe manifests a solution."

"Interesting," I say, feeling my open mind creak shut. "Can the universe manifest me a fresh pizza? I haven't had one since I arrived in Micronesia."

Nat sighs the sigh of a patient teacher tolerating an ignorant student. "Well, Jacques, consider this: a few minutes ago, Nancy and I were a pair of tired, sweaty pedestrians. We wanted to change our situation, so we shifted frequencies, and we manifested YOU."

"Badda-bing, badda-boom!" Nancy intones.

With the assurance of the enlightened, the Norman's flash smug smiles into the rear-view mirror.

My sedan's tires crunch over loose gravel as I pull into the driveway fronting the Crystal Edge Excursions bungalow. SCUBA tanks, lined against the front wall, and a wall mural, highlighting Pohnpei's special dive locations, hint at the establishment's commercial purpose. However, drawn window blinds and an air of vacancy leave us wondering about the business hours.

"Is anybody here?" Nancy wonders.

"Maybe you can manifest the proprietor," I quip.

"Patience," Nat advises.

Emerging from a path alongside the building, at a pace that makes his sandals slap his heels, a teenage boy makes a beeline toward a chest refrigerator situated by the doorway.

"Excuse me!" Nat calls out. "Is this the place for the atoll tour?"

"Ahnd Atoll?" the boy replies. "You hurry, Sir! Boat boarding at dock. Just follow path beside building."

Furrowing his brows, the boy immerses himself in some monumental struggle with the chest refrigerator. Reaching his arms into its depths, he huffs, puffs, readjusts the placement of his feet, and curses in frustration.

"Jacques, do you recognize that voice?" Nat asks.

"The cursing kid?"

"Listen carefully, and you'll hear the universe talking."

"The universe?"

"Right. And, it's showing the way to opportunity and adventure."

"What are you talking about?"

"Didn't you just tell Nancy and me that some days you wished you could get off the island?"

"Sure."

"So, look what's happened. Here you are at a dive outfitter—a place that, until you met us, you never intended to be. Interestingly, there's an excursion boat scheduled for imminent departure. Finally, we see a kid who, judging from his behavior, could use some help bringing something out to the boat. Obviously, the universe heard your wish and arranged before you the circumstances for its fulfillment. Now, are you going to listen to the universe? Don't you want to help that kid?"

Certain the universe has greater priorities than to concern itself with my personal wishes, I sigh cynically, but decide to play along, thinking the chest refrigerator might contain a chilled drink as compensation for my efforts. "Alright," I tell the Normans. "Just for grins." As the Normans head down the path to the dock, I approach the boy.

"Ice chest stuck," the boy explains.

A scab of brown goo, probably the remnants of a soft drink spill, lies congealed around the base of a Coleman tote.

237

With our combined lifting power, the boy and I overcome the goo, and lift the Coleman into the sunlight. Seeing the value of teamwork, the boy gives me a hopeful glance. "Ice chest heavy, Sir. You help carry?"

We lug the Coleman out to the dock. There, the dive boat—a Down-East trawler with a blue hull and orange cabin—wallows in an aroma of diesel. The captain—a mustachioed, beady-eyed fellow carrying a SCUBA tank on deck--exhorts us to a final exertion.

"Ah, there you are, Dino. . .we haven't got all day!" he says. Then, perhaps in deference to a momentarily forgotten customer service protocol, he rushes to assist. "You go relax in cabin, Sir!" he tells me. "Customer don't work for us. . .we work for customer!"

I relax my grip on the tote and step back. In the half voice that I muster as I catch my breath, I mention that I don't have a ticket. The information gets left behind in the boatmen's bustle. A tap on my shoulder distracts me from further pursuit of the matter. "Welcome aboard, Jacques!" Nat Norman enthuses. "When the universe talks, it's best to listen." A smug grin spreads across his face.

"Perhaps you're right," I reply grudgingly, wondering if Nat's lifestyle philosophy might have merit.

Pleased at seeing events unfold as predicted, Nat struts off to join his wife, who leans lazily against the portside railing.

My accidental tourism thus assured, I elect to make myself comfortable, and seek the cold soda that I consider my just reward for helping carry the ice chest. In the forward cabin, I find a handful of passengers in various stages of recline. A square-jawed Frenchman, his torso a sheen of sunscreen, speaks in thickly accented English to other adventurers. From his talk I pluck the names of other Pacific destinations—Palau, Chuuk lagoon, and Vanuatu's Cook Reef—and infer the conversation involves previous dive excursions. Meanwhile, huddled around a duffel bag, several Japanese perform an equipment inventory, sifting through pressure gauges, breath regulators, weight harnesses, and assorted knick-knacks that indicate the seriousness of the venture. Aloof from the crowd, a sketch pad propped upon her knees, a willowy brunette lounges on a cushioned bench. The fine lines that radiate from her eyes and the streaks of gray in her hair hint at a woman well into middle-age, but her smoothly muscled shoulders and ease of posture suggest a youthful energy. Communing with the sketchpad through a charcoal pencil that she holds like a wand, the woman seems to glow with an artistic aura. Casually curious, I crane over her shoulder for a glimpse of her work.

A landscape scene, like a relic from a lost world of light and shadow, fills the page. Though rendered surreal by a curious chiaroscuro, the sketch fleshes the familiar: Sokeh's Rock and Ridge, as seen from across the harbor, a vista reminiscent of my daily commute. Through some quirk of craft, the rendering grants a perspective previously unappreciated, lending Sokeh's basaltic crags a personality not normally associated with inert rock. Entranced by the image, I crane a little too far, and my purloined peep turns rudely intrusive.

"Do you like it?" the artist asks, slightly annoyed.

"It's beautiful," I remark, hoping accolades smooth my lack of decorum.

"Only beautiful?" she presses, sounding disappointed.

"Well, I do sense something. . .how should I say. . ."

"Transcendent?" she suggests.

"Sure," I say. "Transcendent."

"You flatter me," she replies. "I only wish it were true. A Rembrandt might bring out the riddle of the rocks, but I need to sketch a hundred scenes before I come up with something that counts as art. Still, it beats staring at a corporate cubicle."

"There's not much corporate about Sokeh's Ridge," I say. "There's eerie silence, rusting war relics, creepy bugs. . ."

"Like this one?" she remarks, flicking her pencil at a moth flitting across the sketchpad.

"Worse," I say.

We share a laugh, and thinking the conversation suitably ripe for introductions, I venture my name and a handshake.

"Hi Jacques. I'm Uta," she returns.

The exchange of names prods an exchange of glances. At first, I meet her eyes with gentleman confidence. Then, sure that an artist of Uta's caliber must have some deep insight into the way faces reflect character, I feel suddenly self-conscious, afraid that Uta will find in my visage some flaw that renders me unworthy of interest. "Do you ever draw people?" I ask, testing my fears.

"After a fashion," she says, giggling like she delivered the punch-line on a private joke. Thumbing through her sketch pad, she reveals several human renderings—long slender women in hats, in skirts and stiletto heels, in business attire. The more I look, the more the sketches resemble prototypes, their proportions drawn from idealized form. "See, I'm a fashion illustrator," Uta explains.

"You have quite a talent," I remark, recognizing the professional quality of the images.

"I'm a hack," she sighs. "But the money's good." She couches this information in a tone of self-deprecation. During the following conversation, a more detailed biography emerges, and I learn that Uta's financial success came at the cost of an abandoned dream. Trained in the fine arts, she "went corporate" to pay the bills and support a songwriter boyfriend whose music career never got past the demo stage. The pressures of her job left her little time for her artistic passion and infused a mannequin quality into any real portraiture she did attempt. "I can't paint people at all, now," she says. "Not artistically."

240

"What happened to the boyfriend?" I ask

"That didn't work out either."

Still, the corporate life provides a silver lining, Uta tells me. Eager to re-claim the artist within, she takes extended vacations to far-flung parts of the globe, seeking inspirational geography for her new artistic passion: landscapes. "I had a wonderful time in the Sahara," she says. "I spent three weeks sketching the play of light upon the sand dunes."

"So, what brings you to Pohnpei?" I ask.

"My pagan alias," she says. "In the beauty of special places, we find a momentary transcendence that recalls our pagan persona, the source of art."

"What's special about this place?"

"The Luminous Lagoon, of course."

Nearby excursionists glance toward us, as if hearing in our conversation the utterance of a sacred phrase.

"The Luminous Lagoon?" I repeat.

"Oh yes. Ahnd Atoll is famous for it."

"Ah, zee lah-goon ohf lah-eet," the Frenchman intones, nodding. "Much boo-tee-fool."

The Japanese pause their preparations and listen as Uta and the Frenchman provide a preview. Ahnd Atoll, I learn, ranks as a wonder of the diving world, boasting a lagoon of such clarity that sunlight penetrates to incredible depths, revealing coral curiosities elsewhere unseen. The fact that I could dwell on Pohnpei nearly a year and yet remain ignorant of such a place strikes me as an indictment of my character.

A swaying sensation, accompanied by a suddenly more resonant hum, draws my attention back to the dive boat, and I realize that during my conversation with Uta, the boat embarked upon its excursion. Glancing out the window, I see us bob through the shipping channel toward the blue expanse beyond the reef pass. Eager for fresh air, I invite Uta to join me on deck.

We find most of the prime deck-side real estate already occupied, and for lack of a better alternative, settle beside the Normans into a shaded spot along the port railing. For a while I watch the prow splash toward the oblong blob that, interrupting the horizon, signifies the palm-lined shore of Ahnd Atoll. Then, staring back at our wake, I contemplate a different sight: the contours of Pohnpei, which gradually recede to a soundtrack of spray-hiss and engine-drone. Finally, shrunk entirely within a frame of sea and sky, the island poses a primeval panorama, its rainforest slopes an Edenic sanctuary. Yet for all its allure, it seems lonely and forlorn, a green oasis in an empty blue desert, and I marvel that such a limited landscape had defined my life for nearly a year.

"It makes a pretty picture, doesn't it?" Uta says.

"I guess," I brood. "That is, if you can forget about the cholera outbreak."

"Cholera?" Uta asks. The Normans cluster beside us.

"Three dead in Kitti," I continue. "If it spreads into Kolonia, there could be serious trouble. I heard the U.N. might quarantine the island."

"How awful!" Uta exclaims.

"Don't let Jacques ruin your vacation," Nancy Norman intercedes. "He seems to revel in unpleasant information. Earlier, on our way to the dock, he insisted that the cute family we saw riding a motorcycle were really lepers and dog eaters."

"A cloud of dark energy surrounds him," Nat adds, grinning. "We ought to warn you."

"Well Jacques, is this so?" Uta queries, as if giving me the opportunity to confess a crime. "Why do you want to ruin our vacations?"

Though wrapped in a light-hearted tone, the question riles me, and my recent frustrations, augmented by a year's worth of unresolved feelings for my ex fiancée, heave forth. Trumpeting tragedy, I tell the story of my broken heart.

"Ah!" Nancy exclaims. "Now I understand you better."

"You do?" I ask, wiping a tear from my cheek.

"You suffer from *guidance system failure*. The universe is confronting you with the circumstances of your life and asking a question: are you living in accordance with your true purpose?"

"Once, I thought my true purpose was to build a life with Kate. But I'm six-thousand miles away in a cholera outbreak and she's dating another man."

"You feel a sense of loss because you allow limitation to color your perception," Nancy says, her voice soothing and sympathetic. "But is Kate the only one with whom you can build a life?"

"I thought so. . .I thought she was my soul mate."

The Normans smile and wink, hearing in my answer the disillusionment of a child who belatedly discovers the truth about Santa Claus.

"Say rather *a* soulmate," Nancy says. "You fall victim to a limitation mindset when you think you have only one. Get past your limitation."

"How do I do that?" I ask.

"Shift frequencies!" Nat and Nancy chime in unison.

"Lifestyle 2.0 helps you get outside yourself," Nat explains. "You replace your individual identity, the source of your limitation, with abundance—the joy of total being."

"Shift frequencies, discover joy!" Nancy trumpets.

The Normans pause for effect, as though their last utterances contained insight of such significance that it merits a round of applause. Then, apparently satisfied with my lack of reply, and the clueless expression that no doubt accompanies it, they stroll toward the bow to contemplate the approaching atoll.

"Wow! What a couple of freaks!" Uta says. "How did you meet those two?"

"I went to the telecom center," I say matter-of-factly.

As the boat draws nearer the atoll, Uta and I settle our gazes on a deserted beach, peppered, along the high tide line, with coconut husks and driftwood in various states of decomposition. Other than a single-minded commitment to the propagation of the palm tree, a wild ruckus of which sprouts from a carpet of fallen fronds, the landscape presents nothing remarkable. Yet as we drone closer, the boat engine intruding crassly into the silence, I appreciate the sublime symmetry of nature unfettered by human habitation, and sense a beauty beyond the beach, as though the profusion of palms, like the curtains in a theatre, serves to conceal until the proper moment a wondrous attraction. As the dive boat cuts a wake along the atoll's eastern flank, I watch the shoreline slink by, and notice an occasional glimmer through the fabric of trunks. Finally, after we bend toward the southern shore and thread a narrow channel, the curtains part. A pool of radiant blue, so translucent that echoes of sunlight bounce from the deep and spread auroras among the palms, beckons to us.

"The Luminous Lagoon!" the Normans exult.

In deference to the scene, the captain cuts the engine, and we glide forward with the quiet reverence of supplicants entering a temple. Ringed almost entirely by gleaming sand, the lagoon resembles a sapphire in a setting of white gold. Gathering along the boat rail, the passengers marvel at the splendor, which seems to exist for their private appreciation. The thud of the anchor prompts them to head off by ones and twos to don their dive gear.

"Aren't you going to dive?" Uta asks, seeing me hesitate by the rail.

"I'm actually not a diver," I say sheepishly, as though admitting some defect that renders my presence suspect. "I came on this journey by accident."

Uta takes my hand. "Call it a happy accident," she says. "I came to sketch, but first to snorkel. Maybe we can find our

244

pagan personas together."

"Aren't you worried my dark energy might ruin the experience?"

"Oh please. . .don't tell me you actually believe that stuff," Uta admonishes.

We return to the cabin, obtain masks, snorkels, and flippers, and join the assembly of divers on the stern. As I assist Uta in applying sunscreen to her back, divers enter the water, rolling backwards off the stern while keeping a hand on their facemasks. The SCUBA tanks lend an element of swag to the divers' expedition, but Uta displays no sign of equipment envy, and accentuates her unencumbered state by leaping unabashedly from the railing. Once in the water, we secure our masks and snorkels, and, in a gesture of solidarity, hold hands as we embark upon our tour.

Peering into the depths, I develop a strange sensation of falling, an acrophobic reaction to the sight of coral canyons yawning one hundred and fifty feet below. The whoosh of air through my snorkel lends an atmospheric quality to the scene, enhancing my feeling of descent. Though my rational mind recognizes that the forces of flotation remain intact, suspending us like clouds in a liquid sky, I remain disoriented by a defamiliarizing sense of weightlessness.

Uta points below, drawing my attention to a cluster of tadpole shapes that wriggle along a coral wall. When a swarm of gleaming bubbles emanates from the cluster, I recognize the tadpole shapes as divers investigating some benthic attraction. After a slow-motion ascent, the bubbles burst upon our bellies with a tickle.

Inspired by a spontaneous playfulness, Uta and I make a game of the bubbles, swimming into each successive swarm, trying to cap them in our palms, soaring through them with our arms outstretched as wings. Gradually, the strangeness of it all--

the bubbles, the light, and the defamiliarizing weightlessness—
alter my awareness, and the game precipitates a strange
meditation. I perceive the bubbles not as small packages of
exhaled air, but as moments in a continuum of transformation:
though the bubbles fade, the breath continues, returning to the
atmosphere from which it derived. As I center my awareness on
the flow of atmosphere through and around me, my meditation
forms a vision. I see myself as a creature of breath, feather light,
lofted by the convections of the intertropical convergence zone to
the edge of the sky, where a new and different sun reveals the
world as a panorama of possibility. In that moment I believe I
could conjure a cloud and fall as rain on Fern Cove, or spin a storm
and traverse the tropics, or wander the wind, an emissary of the
ether, finding my true dimension beyond time and space. From a
great height I look down upon the luminous lagoon, and I see that

it too resembles a bubble, gleaming in a vast ocean, with me no bigger than a speck of dust on its surface, floating, drifting, a seeker on the threshold of some mysterious insight. Then, the vision shatters, and I find myself in the ordinary world, lit by the ordinary sun.

"Ouch!" Uta shrieks, clasping a hand behind her left knee.

"What happened?" I ask, removing my mask and snorkel.

"Something jabbed my leg!"

For a moment, I think we've drifted into a patch of sea lice, or perhaps a jellyfish. Investigating, I find a plastic minnow fishing lure lodged in the crook of her knee, a crimson stain of blood emanating from where the hook punctured the skin. I deduce that she must have jammed it there when she bent her leg to take a kick, and marvel at the pure bad luck that placed it in her path.

"We better get back to the boat," I advise. "You need some antiseptic."

Uta puts a brave face on the mishap, but after the dive boat captain administers first aid—deftly removing the hook and dousing the wound with Betadine—she succumbs to melancholy. "Is there any place left untainted?" she sighs. "And I've read that even in the middle of the Pacific, a parade of plastic swirls around. Have you heard about it? Scientists call it the Great Pacific Garbage Patch."

Uta's bout with bitterness resurrects my own recent malaise, and I realize that for all its numinous nuance, the lagoon can't dispel an unpleasant fact: when I return to Pohnpei, I'll still be a broken-hearted English teacher stuck in a cholera epidemic. Knowing that misery loves company, Uta and I prop ourselves together against the deck railing, sip sodas, and watch the reflections of the lagoon play upon the ring of palms. In such repose do the Normans find us when they return from their dive.

"What an incredible place!" they chime. "Did you enjoy

your snorkeling expedition?"

"I sought transcendence and discovered trash," Uta says.

"Trash?" Nat questions

"She swam into a fish hook," I explain.

"Don't focus on the fish hook," Nancy Norman advises. "That only traps you in a limitation mindset, which makes you perceive the lagoon according to one small aspect of the experience."

"What should I do?" Uta asks

"Replace the vocabulary of limitation with the vocabulary of abundance," Nat says. "Don't think of the fish hook as 'trash.' Rather, label it according to a more positive connotation —a *tool*, for example.

"Yes, or a bit of *handicraft*," Nancy suggests.

Skeptical, but warming to the wordplay, I too proffer a suggestion. "You could even call it an *artifact*," I add, just for grins.

"Exactly!" Nat enthuses. "An artifact!" Eyes beaming, he drapes an arm over my shoulder, like a sage mentor taking a neophyte apprentice under his wing, and tells me I've taken the first step to a larger understanding.

Excerpt from a Diary, May 2000

Sunday brunch, the Village Hotel—I join personnel from various departments for an informal gathering before summer break and travel plans scatter us around the globe. Our casual demeanor, added to the hotel's amiable charm, suggests a lighthearted spirit, but can't fully sugarcoat an unpleasant truth: the cholera outbreak has us on edge. The knowledge that members of our own students' families count among the victims lends the crisis an emotional proximity too overbearing for some. Margaret, a New Zealander two months into her contract as librarian, considers the "perils of Pohnpei" too much for her toddler child and announces her plans to return home as soon as she can make arrangements.

Gavin, ever the wisecracker, thinks the "Perils of Pohnpei" would make a great book title, calling it "alliterative and intriguing."

Fred Knox, the elder statesman of the Lang/Lit Department, suggests that one of us should write a book about the island. "There are some real interesting characters here, with some interesting stories," he asserts.

Gavin nods his agreement, and volunteers Jasper for the task, noting the fascinating quality of Jasper's journey from small-town bookstore clerk to Chair of the Lang Lit Dept., family man, and expert on Pohnpeian clan culture. "It would be a transformative journey of the human spirit, set in an exotic locale," he grins.

"Oh, that sounds interesting!" Katy Jones says. "I'd read that book!"

Jasper smirks, unsure if his story really counts as a transformative journey. "Maybe Gavin should write his own autobiography," Jasper suggests.

"What would your book be about, Gavin?" Katy asks.

"I'd tell the story of a hotel management consultant whose

savoir faire and magnetic personality opened access to the inner circles of expat intrigue. It would be a psychological thriller, but with enough romance and hijinks to keep mainland audiences interested."

"That sounds great!" Katy says. "I'd read that book! And how about you, Jacques? What kind of book would you write?"

I ponder the question as the collective gaze of the table regards me expectantly. To my mind comes a recollection of my bungled lesson plans, failed attempts at romance, and emotional turmoil resulting from unresolved feelings for my ex-fiancée. Then, I think about the characters I met and the waves I rode.

"I'd write a book about an English teacher who had a broken heart, but then met some cool people and went surfing," I say.

"That doesn't sound like a very good book," Katy frowns.

"Why not?" I ask, surprised by her disappointment.

"Well, for one thing, there aren't any beaches here," Katy explains. "A good story requires a good setting. How can you have a surfing adventure in a place with no beaches?"

Murmurs and nods ripple around the table. Then Jasper adds a cynical editorial: "I tried to tell him that when I picked him up at the airport last August. When I saw a surfboard among his luggage, I thought, 'Are we sure we want to hire this guy? What a nutcase!'"

Epilogue: Rainbows and Unicorns

The job interview in Santa Maria, an agricultural hub located alongside Highway 101 in California's central coast, lasts from mid-morning through late afternoon. Conducted by faculty whose ivy-league attitude seems pretentious in rural California, the interview involves a teaching demo, campus tour, and Q&A

before a ten-person committee. Still off-kilter from the blur of wings and wheels that whisked me from Micronesia to California, I stumble through the process, my suit-and-tie exterior at odds with an inner-self still on island time. My anecdotes about teaching in Micronesia make the dour professoriate regard me more as a specimen of curiosity than a worldly professional, and by the time the interview concludes, my optimism at being a first-round candidate—no small achievement for a job opening that probably drew two-hundred applications—gives way to feelings of inadequacy. Afterward, on the way to my car, I catch my reflection in an office window, and think the suit-and-tie visage gazing back from the glass belongs not to me, but rather an alternate reality vision, a doppelganger haunting a parallel universe but not yet ready to materialize.

Returning to my car, I exchange my suit for street clothes and the relaxed persona of a teacher on summer break. Thinking a surf session would help me get into character—and with my surf gear packed for just such a purpose—I contemplate a quick drive north to Pismo Beach. However, the velocity of the wind, funneled from the Pacific into the Santa Maria Valley, convinces me that instead of crisp beach-break spinners I'd only find ragged wind-chop. With plans to see my parents later in Los Angeles, I set off south. After living on an island whose haphazard roads preclude speeds greater than 30 mph, I relish the sense of freedom that comes from pushing the speedometer to 70 and feeling the warm valley air billow past my ears. To the east, hillsides draped with vineyards roll past in gentle undulations. To the west, oak woodlands spread pools of tree-shade over meadows of yellow grass and evoke a time when the road bore a Spanish name, El Camino Real, the route of Franciscan priests who traveled on horseback between mission settlements. Thinking about the missions makes me consider the people who helped build them —the indigenous Californians, including the Chumash, who once roamed the area and possibly gathered acorns from the very oaks I now pass. Picturing my place in the grand sweep of history, I romanticize the road, viewing it with the appreciation of an exile who indulges in sentimentality upon the sight of familiar lands. Mirroring my mood, the afternoon sun infuses the hills with a warm, fuzzy sense of communion. The rapture lasts until a passing RV, towing behind it a Jeep and trailer full of motorcycles, re-acquaints me with the insistent hum of late-stage capitalism. Sadly, I picture a future in which the oak-dotted hills succumb to subdivisions.

In Buellton I stop for gas. A moment of comic disorientation occurs when I pay the cashier and drive off, forgetting to pump the gas. When I see the gas gauge remain near "empty," I realize my mistake and return post-haste to the fortunately vacant pump. Afterward, downplaying my momentary confusion—a symptom that an experienced veteran of jet lag might recognize as a harbinger of severe functional impairment—I naively continue the drive, unaware of the disruption that long flights from west to east, such as the one I recently undertook, inflict upon the circadian rhythm. The full effect of this disruption hits me on a lonely stretch of highway before the Nojoqui Summit. One moment, I register the mundane scenery of a summer evening: a field of wild mustard, yellow flowers quivering; a distant truck, curving in to the ascent before the Gaviota Pass; a fading sun, striking my mirrors with shafts of amber light. Then I register nothing, as I suddenly fall asleep at the wheel.

Roused from sleep by the jolt of car tires on a highway rumble strip, I experience the unique stimulation of driving off the road at freeway speed. Primed with adrenaline, I swerve away from the onrushing foliage and bounce along the dirt partition—a particularly uneven surface which tests the resiliency of the shock absorbers and knocks my head against the

253

doorframe. Pumping the brakes, I come to a halt. Heart-in-mouth, I take a deep breath, my brain oscillating between survival-mode panic and objective awareness. Once my pulse settles down, I place the transmission in "park" and step out to survey the vehicle. Other than a new-found appreciation for the thin margin which separates the mundane from the mortifying, the incident leaves no mark, and I return to the road. Ironically, the knowledge that I could fall asleep at any moment makes me strangely alert, at least temporarily, and I manage the Gaviota Pass without difficulty. At Gaviota Landing, where the highway rejoins the coast, I decide not to tempt fate any further and pull into a rest stop. Reclined in the back of my vehicle, with my wetsuit as a pillow, I settle in to sleep, my fitful dreams infused with the odor of old neoprene.

When I wake, the sweet scent of coastal sage, carried by the night breeze, wafts through the window gaps. I clamber outside, stretch, and make my way to the restroom, where pale lights illuminate the only other vehicle in the parking lot, a jacked-up Ford F-150 with balloon-style knobby tires. The truck sports Oregon plates and a window sticker that reads "bow hunters do it with longer shafts." Projecting rugged individualism on a chassis of muscular machinery, the truck seems to assert the belief, prevalent in American road culture, that vehicle choice enhances personal identity. The driver, standing beside a vending machine against the bathroom wall, cigarette in hand, adheres to the survivalist image I expect, his halfway buttoned flannel revealing a chest tattooed with a "death spade"—a skull within an ace-of-spades insignia. The pulse of speed metal, emanating from the cab's interior, confirms the character, or so I think. When a dainty dollop of a dog, its beady eyes like black buttons on a white mop, barks at me from the dashboard, I reconsider.

"Sparky!" the man admonishes. "Quiet down!" As I

approach, he offers a shrug of apology. "Don't mind little Sparky. Poor thing, he's got the aspirations of a Doberman, but he's trapped in the body of a Maltese Terrier."

The incongruity of the dainty dog and the testosterous truck jars my perception. Suspicious that Sparky represents a public relations prop, a cute companion to soften the man's edgy persona, I keep my guard up. Then, troubled by my rush to judgement, I wonder if my return to the mainland exposed me to a simultaneous revival of mainland stereotypes. For all I know the bowhunter represents a modern incarnation of Buddha, possessing wisdom worthy of enlightenment.

When I exit the bathroom, Sparky responds with a hesitant yip, barely audible over the sound of Metallica's "Master of Puppets" thumping through the truck's door speakers. The bowhunter, immersed in a rapture of air guitar, indeed offers wisdom, forgotten during my year of radio-free island life: on a long drive, nothing helps pass the time like rock 'n roll.

Back in my car, I turn on the radio. Accelerating out of the rest stop, I rejoin the 101 as it shoots past Gaviota Landing and runs parallel to the Santa Barbara Channel. Free of the stifling hills, the radio rejoices with receptivity, and quickly pulls in some up-tempo tunes, beamed from an L.A. station. Meanwhile, a rising moon, nearly at its full, paints silver sparkles on the sea and illuminates the horizon with enough clarity that I decipher the silhouettes of oil platforms situated between Santa Barbara and the Channel Islands. Refreshed from my nap, grooving on music and moonlight, I feel newly alive, and when the speakers sound the bass line from The Doors' "L.A. Woman," its 8th note rhythm like a pagan pulse, I mime the drumbeat by slapping my palms on the steering wheel, hearing in the song an anthem for my homeward push.

Surging south, I take in the serene loneliness, interrupted by an occasional Coleman Lantern at a State Beach campground,

255

that settles on the Gaviota Coast at night. The road wends past UCSB, and the moonlight reveals a subdued hint of the red tile charm that compels many to regard Santa Barbara as the quintessence of the California Dream. With artful lane changes, I skirt a minor traffic tangle, and soon put the town in my rear-view mirror. I pass Montecito, where stands of Eucalyptus shroud the estates of the California Riviera, and cruise through Carpinteria, scene, in my youth, of many winter surf sojourns. When I encounter the sign for Bates Road, I decelerate to a more leisurely pace, the better to glimpse Rincon Point, its iconic cove the site of so much surfing lore. There, from stream to seawall, the sea glows platinum, lapping the cobblestone shore. Absent the corduroy texture of a groomed west swell—rare in summer—the scene lacks a key inspirational element, but nevertheless, the sight of California's fabled winter point break kindles a nostalgic longing for California point surf, inspiring a mental roll-call of the spots I now pass: Oil Piers, Ventura Overhead, C-Street. Through Oxnard, the smell of fertilizer replaces the sea-tang, and the moonlight gleams on rows of agricultural sheeting. Eager to continue my point-break panegyric, I take a side road across the fields, eventually finding the Pacific Coast Highway and the coastline I crave. At Pt. Mugu, where the road snakes through a blasted gap in the eroding outcrop of the point, I feel like I've passed through a portal to a luminous land. The moonlight, amplified by its reflection off the sand dunes behind Thornhill Broome State Beach, simply dazzles, priming my pagan impulse—a sentiment that grows when, at County Line, I see the tell-tale lines of a small south swell. "Night surfing!" I think.

Requiring a special combination of circumstances—bright moon, clear sky, proper tide, and decent swell—night surfing thrills in large part because of its rarity. Still, the thrill comes with an eerie quality, as seascapes that seem alluring by day may develop demons after dark. Gurgles and sudden shadows suggest finned predators; murky depths shroud jagged rocks; and the beach itself attracts dubious characters, whose adherence to law and order diminishes with the lateness of the hour. Accordingly, I seek comfort of my "home" break, Topanga Point. At the intersection of L.A.'s canyon/urban interface, it provides a focal point both for swell energy and a crew of "regulars" who find its quick right slides a fun release from the gripes of the Grid. For years a member of this demographic, I retain an encyclopedic memory of the point's quirks and tendencies, and so make Topanga my preferred arena for moonlight missions. Musing on the memory of those missions, I wonder if any "night crew" friends might already be in the water.

Rising and descending across bluffs and ravines, the highway brings me past the western end of Santa Monica Bay. A vista opens, and a string of twinkling lights fills my windshield. Extending from Malibu to Palos Verdes, the vista reveals the beachside bulwark of the vast L.A. city-scape that glows behind. Among those lights await family, friends, projects, and possibilities, facets of a life with which I long to reconnect. But not just yet, for the moonlight calls, offering a prospect of surf, whose quality I confirm when I pass Malibu Point, where south swell lines trace a foamy fizzle, like gossamer spun from moonlight, along the 1st Point cove. Pushing on, the highway follows the seaward thrust of the Santa Monica Mountains' sedimentary knuckles, skirts the mouths of canyons that yawn between moon-glossed hills, and shakes off a cluster of beachfront bungalows, bringing me to the doorway of my desideratum, Topanga Point.

A light breeze blows across the highway, wafting an odor of fish-fry from the trash bins of the Reel Inn, a seafood restaurant situated opposite the beach parking lot. The neon sign above the restaurant crackles and buzzes, as if voicing displeasure with the smell. Meanwhile, I voice displeasure with my wetsuit, as with grunts and contortions I try to cajole the stale neoprene around my body. Finally, having tamed the reluctant rubber, I grab my board, lock the car, and trot down the stairs to the beach, where the moonlight curiously transforms the familiar landmarks, making the lifeguard shack a beach pagoda, the palm tree a mysterious obelisk, and the guano-coated sand by the creek a blanket of powdered sugar. Skirting a congregation of seagulls that, heads tucked on wings, repose by the creek mouth, I step gingerly across the rocks at the top of the point. Acclimated to the tropics, I wince at the initial chill of water that seeps against my skin. Wading in to the surf, I lie prone on my board and begin paddling, each stroke a further immersion into a mystical realm where instinct and adrenaline channel perception.

Once in the take-off zone, I discover I have company, a dread-locked, bearded surfer whose black wetsuit and green-gray board blend into the shadows. "Any good ones?" I ask, invoking, through the question, a recognition of our common purpose.

"Always!" he says, his whiskers giving way to a display of white teeth that I take for a grin. "It's rainbows and unicorns out here, bro!"

"Rainbows and unicorns? That sounds interesting." Paddling close, I extend a handshake. "I'm Jacques," I say.

"I'm Bruno," he says, returning the introduction.

A wave materializes from the moonlight. Bruno sprint-paddles to the peak, and I offer a complimentary hoot as he drops in. Like a genie on a flying carpet, he passes by with a whoosh, levitating through the moon-glow toward the darkness of the cove. A second wave follows, the ripples on its crest like scintillating silver scales. Stroking past strands of kelp that slither under the surface, I stand and race a vortex of light and shadow down the point, the hiss of water under my board accompanied by ululations from the cove as Bruno hoots me on.

Through the night, backlit by the westering moon, the

waves turn progressively more ethereal, and our passage upon them increasingly like an initiation into some sublime mystery. Eventually, during a lull between sets, we pick up the thread of conversation.

"Malibu could be good tomorrow," I opine.

"It'll be better at night," Bruno says.

"Think so? The mid-day tide will be perfect for Malibu."

"It's been years since I've surfed in daylight, at Malibu or anywhere else," Bruno replies. "I only surf at night."

"Seriously? You only surf at night?" The information takes me aback, and I wonder how anyone with a passion for surfing could be content with such a limited window for its pursuit.

"I've acclimated," Bruno explains. "I've trained myself to see even by the light of half a moon. And it's transformed my appreciation for surfing."

"How so?" I ask.

"Well, just look at us. . . to be in this place, at this time, with these waves, soaring on moonbeams while everyone else shuts themselves in boxes. . .You realize that night surfing is a gift, an invitation to live keenly in a world that constantly tries to dull your edge," Bruno explains. "At night, even mediocre waves become special, magical moments."

"Ah. . .Rainbows and unicorns?" I deduce.

"Exactly."

"You're quite a philosurfer."

"Very punny," Bruno says, riposting my joke.

"So how about you?" he asks. "What brings you out here?"

"I guess I just happened to be driving by at the right time. Actually, I'm trying to find my bearings and get over a case of jet lag."

"Jet lag? Where have you been?"

"Micronesia. I've been living on an island for nearly a year, teaching English."

"No kidding! What was that like? Get any surf?"

The question makes me ponder the entirety of my experience. Gazing out to sea, I let my mind's eye follow the moon path, over the horizon and across the Pacific. I imagine the island of Pohnpei, its contours caressed by the moon's soft, ethereal glow. From that glow, scenes emerge, sketches gleaned from my year of Micronesian waves and wanderers. Appreciating the circumstances that put me in that place, at that time, among those waves, I regard my journey as a gift, an inspiration to live as keenly as possible.

"Rainbows and unicorns," I say, hearing in Bruno's philosophy a motto for the experience. "It was rainbows and unicorns."

"Awesome!" he says.

A glimmer up the point signals an approaching set wave, and we stroke to greet it, angling for the peak.

PhantaSea Books

Fascinating tales of historical intrigue, cultural curiosity, and travel adventure

I Fell in Love with an Aleutian Vampire. A tale of love, war, and the power of faith. Author Quinn Haber relates the saga of Lieutenant Jake Harper, whose WWII assignment entailed a foray behind enemy lines in the far North Pacific, into a realm of enduring twilight and even more enduring mystery.

The Somali Pirate. A tale of struggle at the intersection of subsistence living and international politics. In this book, the first in a three-part series, Quinn Haber presents the story of Noor Fayrus, whose induction into the pirate life provides a new perspective on the complex issue of piracy near the Horn of Africa.

The Somali Pirate 2. The adventures of Noor Fayrus of the Darod Clan continue in *Dagger Dogs of Zayid*, Quinn Haber's sequel to *The Somali Pirate.* Unexpected twists and intriguing characters make this a compelling narrative for readers enamored of traditional pirate tales.

The Somali Pirate 3: White Star Empire. In this action-packed conclusion to the Somali Pirate series, author Quinn Haber depicts how the Dagger Dogs' effort to improve their lives pits them against entrenched powers whose interests prove antithetical to a better Somalia. *White Star Empire* provides "insights about Somali Culture, unconventional justifications for Somali piracy, and just the right touch of fantasy" — Kirkus Reviews.

The Volcano Trilogy: A Philippines Surfing Odyssey. A classic tale of travel-adventure from prolific author Quinn Haber. Surfing, romance, and culture-shock combine in a riveting three-part travelogue.

Tonkin. France, 1889—Paris pulses in anticipation of the World's Fair. In this tale of high society, anarchists, and beasts, author Quinn Haber depicts a historical moment in which dark forces pursue a terrible agenda.

Echoes from the Sun: A Modern Quest for the Fountain of Youth. Writer, poet, and global adventurer Ari Marsh blends archeology, history, and religion in a tale that confronts the esoteric mysteries of life. From the mountains of Baja California to the cities of Europe, the narrative follows a young traveler whose discovery of an ancient amulet launches him on a life-changing journey of the spirit.

The Heart of a Traveler: Reflections from the Fathomless Edge of the World. Through this collection of vignettes, sketches, and poetry based on his global adventures, author Ari Marsh takes readers on a journey of light and darkness, from Bali to Peru, from love to death, and toward the unparalleled exhilaration of gliding across rolling swells of liquid turquoise.